ENDORSEMENTS

This is a success story that should be shared with many. There are millions of people struggling with various types of "good intentions." The true stories from Steve provide insights and experiences that will change lives for the good. Today, Steve's son and daughter are as close as they can be to their father. This is a good life story that should be read, believed and followed on the path Steve discovered.

—**Milt McKenzie**
Businesses Investor and Entrepreneur

Since 2006 I have worked side by side with Steve in the United States and all over North America. As he took sales representatives on a journey of self-discovery and awareness during his training, he guided them to realize their own "aha" moment and did it by creating a path of interest, curiosity and desire, which brought about their new job experiences.

—**Ken Burgdorf**
Former Director of Training & Development
for Culligan International

I both laughed and cried at all the different ways I have led my life *Blinded by Good Intentions*. Steve's incredible true story will help you understand "the middle path" and find a better way to happiness, peace, and healing through Christ.

—**Michael Carricarte**
President, Int'l Major Medical
Pan American Private Client

BLINDED
by GOOD
INTENTIONS

*Because Your Best
Intentions May Be
Your Worst Enemy*

STEVE WHITE

WinePressPublishing
Great Books, Defined.

WinePress Publishing (PO Box 428, Enumclaw, WA 98022) functions only as book publisher. As such, the ultimate design, content, editorial accuracy, and views expressed or implied in this work are those of the author.

Unless otherwise noted, all Scriptures are taken from the *Holy Bible, New International Version®, NIV®*. Copyright © 1973, 1978, 1984 by Biblica, Inc.™ Used by permission of Zondervan. All rights reserved worldwide. www.zondervan.com

ISBN 13: 978-1-4141-1985-4
ISBN 10: 1-4141-1985-2
Library of Congress Catalog Card Number: 2010940634

The book was written for and is dedicated to my son Ian and daughter Kari, and to my friend's children who walked through life with us all: Dan, David, and Beth.

You are all deeply loved and greatly appreciated.

CONTENTS

FOREWORD
MY DAD REALLY WAS A JERK!

This book has saved my relationship with my father. At 14, I had written him off completely, ran away from home, began selling drugs and quickly adopted the lifestyle that comes with life disasters. It's been one hell of a roller coaster ride since then and for many of those years, I disregarded my father's role in my life to nothing more than a pain in my ..., fortunately though, this isn't where our story ended!

This book is for you if ...

- If you are frustrated with relationships
- If you are disappointed with how people treat you
- If you find yourself engaged in disagreements with others
- If you wonder why things don't work out as you intended
- If you have reoccurring thoughts that you're not good enough
- If you have unfulfilled expectations for life

- If you have experienced setbacks, or have failed in life by always messing up
- If you keep doing what you think is right but it's not working for you
- If you have reoccurring thoughts of how others have wronged you
- If you find yourself reviewing and replaying the faults of others

In the book, you'll read stories of my dad's journey through his good intentions. You'll learn how being blinded by the good intentions led him to the loss of his wife, daughter, the fall of his son, destruction of his life's plan and ultimately to the discovery of grace, freedom and redemption from those good intentions. Many of these stories seem either "too bad" or "too outlandish" to be true. In both cases, I can assure you that everything you're about to read is fact. Although I've seen him at his worst, it is through the writing of this book—his life's story, that I can proudly say that I now see him at his best.

Thank you, Dad, for your ability to share some of your most private and trying circumstances so openly and humbly. Thank you for always loving me even while I wandered so far. I trust this book will bring healing and restoration to countless families, relationships and individuals who are struggling due to their own "good intentions." It has for me.

—**Ian White**
He is the son of the author.
He lives in Colorado near his dad.

From the daughter: In this book, my dad tells stories about how he lost his children, his marriage, and the life he wanted with his good intentions. It's all true! I was there through much of the worst of it and the fall out. It's been a rough road and there were years I had written my dad off and told him never to speak to me again. But the beauty of this book is it is not only the candid nature of which he tells in the stories, but also the principles that led him back to the life he now lives. A life that I desire ... so much so, that not only am

I reunited with him as a daughter, but he has also become my most trusted mentor. It has been very insightful and I have worked to base my life in what you'll find within this book and it has made me a better wife, mother, daughter, and friend. I can now say something wholeheartedly that I never believed I would be saying; "my dad is my hero". Thank you dad for living your life openly and honestly! And thank you for what this book offers each of us; a new way to live that releases us from being "Blinded by Good Intentions." I believe this book is great for all families.

—**Kari Stowe**
She is the author's daughter.
She's a mom and wife in Mesa Arizona.

PREFACE

Why is the book in your best interest?
- We need and want to know what causes bad life issues,
- We want the truth of how to prevent bad life outcomes.
- We love gaining proof of the way to make our life the best.

Why you would invest time in the book?
- To learn how to make life improvements work out.
- We can't learn everything in a few minutes, we need time to read and re-read and remember.
- We wasted time the wrong way, now we want to use time the best way.

This book is the true story of my life, what I discovered was wrong with me, and how I walked through all of life's disasters.

I had good intentions and much ambition. But for a long time, something prevented me from seeing and learning what was off track, and why my game plan wasn't working. My intentions were probably a lot like everyone else's. I wanted to be a great husband, parent, friend, worker, and a success story. These were my life goals, and I considered them worthy. But at one time or another, they all failed. I learned that our best intentions can become our worst enemies when we are blind to why they are not working. And I learned that plans fail not necessarily because one's intentions are bad, but rather that their success or failure hinges on how the plans are executed.

What I discovered about my failures is one motive for writing *Blinded by Good Intentions*. I lost my hopes and dreams—and the hopes and dreams of my family. I lost almost everything of any value. I want to reveal what I discovered through these experiences so that others might learn from my failures and minimize their own losses. The insights and solutions I discovered were earned the hard way: I experienced them. My defeats were heart-breaking, but perhaps the price I paid will protect others.

All the stories are true; some even appeared in newspapers. My experiences reflect the frog in the kettle syndrome. If you put a frog in hot water, he will jump out. But if you put a frog in cold water and then gradually turn up the heat, the frog will stay until it is cooked to death. My life has been like that frog, and I can tell you that once the water starts boiling, it may be too late to change the situation or escape without great damage.

Are you, as I was, in a slowly heating pot? My stories may help you realize—before you lose those you love and all the things that lead to peace and joy—that some changes are necessary.

I assume you have good intentions for yourself and others. Hopefully this book will prevent people from being blinded by good intentions and seeing their hopes and dreams abandoned by the wayside. If you have already lost your hopes and dreams, and feel nothing you sought will ever become a reality, I want you to know that I got everything back (except my wife). In the end I experienced peace, comfort, and the healing of my broken heart. The same can happen to you.

When it comes to the power of life stories, we are not alone. Our stories are different, but they are relevant and powerful, not only for ourselves but also for others. Discovering your own story by reading mine could have an incredible effect as you go forward. I hope that it does.

And like reviewing your own journal entries, re-reading some of these stories that connect to yours, over a few months, will help you gain more insights.

How the Book Unfolds

The sequence of these stories follows the path I took discovering what went wrong with my life and how I experienced change. The stories themselves reveal the ways I was unaware of my intentions, life rules, vows, and commitments. Some of the stories show the right path of life; some show the wrong path. Others reveal how changes happened and how they made my life better, regardless of what else was going on in my world.

I discovered the difference between holding intellectual concepts in my mind and having character in my heart. I felt the former would change me, but it didn't. What brought a real change from within was heart-change. I thought my intellect would guide me on the right track and control my behaviors, but I found in the long run that it brings only surface changes. When pressures mounted, the bad patterns I thought I'd conquered came back with a vengeance.

I tried to look and sound good on the outside by using the right words and by meeting the standards of a good person. But I was blind to what was happening inside. I put blinders over my heart and eyes because my mind told me that, with my good intentions, I knew what I was doing. Much of what I learned about the truth came from experiencing failures that exposed problems within me, things I could no longer explain away intellectually. My experience with failure—and learning from it—made the dramatic difference. It was as great as the difference between actual fruit growing on a tree and ornaments that look like fruit hanging on a tree.

Though dramatic, the change took time. The process of finding the solutions to my problems was as important as the solutions themselves.

A Few Other Considerations About the Book

A close friend is a counselor who finds that husbands are often blind to the fact that their marriage is failing. They are shocked when the ???? hits the fan because they love their wives and think they have been doing everything possible to be good husbands. My friend also finds that wives think it's their prerogative to try to change their husbands. So they keep reminding their husbands what they should be doing and wearing and saying. Rather than nagging, they see this as expressing good intentions for the benefit of the marriage.

At times I was sure nothing would change things, so I never expected change. I tried everything, but ultimately it proved useless. This state of affairs also kept me from being open-minded about different perspectives. I was willing to suffer extreme pain and frustration, so long as I could tell myself that I was full of good intentions—and so long as I was committed to being a "manly man."

When my world accelerated out of control, negative thoughts kept me from real wisdom. There were times I was not worried about my problems, and I didn't really care to think about them. If they worked out, then fine. But if not, it was no big deal. That seemed like a good attitude at the moment, but it prevented me from learning. So my problems became chronic.

In the middle of this book I ask, "What was God's part in all of this?" The book is not about religiosity and all the *shoulds, shouldn'ts, do's,* and *don'ts.* I offer insights from the Bible, but I am not writing about any particular formal religion or even exclusively about Christianity. It is about real experiences with God.

Whether you believe in God is a different question from whether you believe in religion. Christ himself was disgusted with religiosity and those who lived that way. To me, that makes total sense. I think you will be surprised and encouraged at what happened to me and the experiences I write about. I reveal things about myself very openly, so these pages include the good, the bad, and my experiences with the Heavenly Father. The last thing I want to do is encourage anyone to become a religious weirdo.

Yes, I lost my family, my hopes, my dreams, and a lot of other things of value. But during it all I came to discover a deeper relationship with God. I had been a "Christian" for decades, but through my difficulties there came an incredible change between God and me—a change that continues to this day.

SECTION 1

IN THE
BEGINNING

HOUSTON, WE HAVE A PROBLEM!

Ten years into my marriage, at age thirty-eight, an event happened that gave me a particular insight about my intentions. I learned something from what happened, so I wanted to change and make things work better. But it took about five more years for me to discover all that was preventing my good intentions from working to the good. Sometimes the way we gain insights is not the way we would choose. That was certainly so in this case.

Because I wanted to improve as a dad and husband, I asked my family their opinion about me. I first went out to the front yard, where my daughter, who was seven, was playing. "I would like to ask you a question," I said, "and I want a true answer. I promise I won't get mad if you tell me the truth. Honey, what do you think I am like as your dad?"

Instantly she responded, "Dad, you're a macho, know-it-all jerk!"

I took a step backward. This was not what I expected! I thanked her for her honesty and stormed into the house.

A minute later I saw my son and asked him the same question. He said exactly what his sister had. Now I was angry. I thought he had talked to my daughter and coached her what to say. *Those were his words,* I thought, *not hers.* = I stomped off to find my wife.

I told Deb what had just happened and what the kids said.

To the best of my memory, this is exactly what she said: "You _____, of course you're a jerk. Haven't I been telling you this for years?" Then she stomped off.

If their reactions were even *close* to accurate, then obviously something was very wrong with me. I had been blind to how I was doing as a husband and father. But for how long?

Instead of getting mad at me for how I duped myself, I got mad at my family for what they said. Yet as I thought about it, I became more subdued. The candid comments from three loved ones helped me realize I needed to change my lifestyle. Clearly, my good intentions were not working! I felt like the astronaut in the movie *Apollo 13* when he said, "Houston, we have a problem."

But I did eventually find that over time, changes to the good became real.

Good Intentions Are Not the Problem

Change can and does come. I came up with some of my best intentions when I was only twelve. I wanted to be a great father and a great husband! I also wanted to be a manly man. To me that meant I would be great at my job, live life in a good way, and do the things that needed to be done. Even at the age of twelve, I was serious about my commitment to those intentions. Being a great husband and dad are good intentions, and I thought they would result in me loving, honoring, having compassion, and cherishing my wife and children. It may seem odd that a boy would have these concerns, but I had specific reasons for my intentions. I will tell you about them in some of the stories. For now, suffice it to say that for a long time, my good intentions did not work out.

My stories span the time from my youth to my current age. They will include the experiences, exposures, realizations, and insights that caused me to be blinded by my good intentions. The new discoveries and experiences brought me a new attitude that helped me gain freedom from my old patterns. Gaining that freedom has brought peace, joy, excitement, and a sense of life as an adventure.

It's All True

My good intentions about being a great husband and dad remained my overriding goal. My other intentions were also good, but somehow the way I had, for decades, carried them out left me in ruins. Deb left me in 2000, taking my daughter with her. At that time my son was in jail. It was definitely time for me to turn things around. I was open to receiving insights and eager to experience changes. The stories that follow will show that even though one is blinded by good intentions, things can still work out and lead to a healthy, positive, peaceful, and joyful outcome.

LIFE'S EVENTS

I remember most of the details of my life's events. I also remember the rules I lived by and the vows I made. Through it all, I maintained intentions I thought were good. I always assumed that good intentions would keep me on the right track and make life better. For almost forty years I didn't realize that rules, regulations, and good intentions can sneak in, take over, and put us on the wrong track.

I remember the first time I thought good intentions would put me on the right track. While in the fifth grade, I lived in Garden Grove, in Southern California, in a neighborhood like you would have seen on the TV show *Leave it to Beaver*. I had great friends who all went to the same school. Eisenhower Elementary was just down the street, and I loved it—mainly because my friends and I were the most popular guys at school, and the best athletes.

Scott, Mike W., Mike P., Dale, Mark, and Peter were my best friends. We spent most of our time at sports. Weekends were great; we played baseball, football, and basketball year 'round. And our talents did not go unnoticed. Because of our local reputation and how well we played basketball together, we even got invited to play during an NBA halftime once in Los Angeles. It was just a ten-minute game, so they chose only five of the seven of us. Since I was the smallest, I didn't get picked. It devastated my attitude and self-worth. That was the first chink in my armor, but there would be more.

After school I spent most of the time at my friends' homes. There was no real reason for me to go home; my dad was nonexistent. I have only one vague memory about him while I was growing up: We went camping as a family at a lake once. I do not remember where he was, or why he was never around the house when my mom worked full-time. She was a cop—or at least she worked in the cop shop (as we called the police department back then). Since no adult was around to catch us, about the only reason to go to my house was to sneak a smoke or do other stuff we weren't supposed to do.

Somewhere in this time, my parents got divorced. I didn't even know they were in the process. In fact, I don't remember much about my parents' relationship, except that there wasn't one. That was obviously because my dad had been absent from the family almost all the time. I found out later that their split had been in process for years.

This is an instance when life rules can sneak in and take over good intentions. In the 1960s, divorce was not acceptable. And when a divorce happened, people reacted in a negative way. One of my friends told me his parents didn't want him hanging around me anymore. They decided I came from an immoral family and would have a bad influence. So I was no longer allowed to come into their home. They probably had good intentions—thinking they were protecting their son from hanging out with a loser—but it didn't sit well with me.

The parents of the rest of my close friends took the same approach, except for Scott's folks. Scott lived farther away, and, as I found out years later, his folks were having their own marital troubles. During sports at school, none of my friends would pick me first to be on their team anymore. Instead I was picked last. Feeling hurt, embarrassed, and mad, I lost interest in sports.

Humiliation and shame pushed me to find a new set of friends. Instead of playing sports, these new friends spent most of their time getting into trouble. They were seen as losers—just like me. We started hanging around together and doing some pretty bad stuff. I'm too embarrassed to tell you the things we did; even today I might get thrown in jail!

I became just the sort of kid others had projected me to be—a loser! I was angry at life and everyone around me. I did things with my new friends that fed off my anger.

Those things became my adventures, and I used them to take my mind off all the things that were going wrong. Those adventures included things like playing with fire, causing explosions, launching things, burning things, torturing things, and getting into a lot of fights. I wasn't very successful as a fighter, due to my size, and I got pounded regularly. I wore my attitude on my sleeve and became like a human magnet for idiots who wanted to pick on someone. These kinds of adventures pretty much represented an average day for me and my friends. They made us laugh.

Manly Man

After my parents' divorce, I started junior high school. Because I was one of the smallest guys at school, the biggest guy—a real jerk—always picked on me. He was in my wood shop class, and every day he would slap me on the back of my head. One day, he slapped the back of my head while he was wearing a huge ring. It felt like he hit me with a hammer. That made me so mad, I punched him in the face. I took my fist and brought it as far back as I could reach, so I would hit him as hard as possible. I had to jump up while swinging, and I hit him in the bottom of the jaw. That knocked him backwards and he tripped and hit his head on a wooden table, which knocked him out. Apparently I was the only one who saw his head hit the table. Everyone, including him, thought I had knocked him out with my punch!

No one liked this bully, and in an instant I became "the manly man." Everyone was cheering, and even the teacher seemed happy because he knew this guy had been slapping me. When the guy regained consciousness, he was terrified. He never picked on me again, and his whole attitude in school changed. From that time on he actually became friendly toward me.

So getting the best of the bully was good. As far as I was concerned, hitting him was a good thing. But that event led me down the road of believing that anger was the way to control people and situations. And that is not a good thing.

A Failure at Life

Another set of events involved my aunt. A tall blonde, she was considered a hot babe in those days. After my parents' divorce I would often go to my grandmother's house, and at times my aunt and uncle were there. For years she would pull me aside and tell me that because I came from a divorced family, people would understand why I would fail at life. I can't remember how many times she told me I would be a loser and a failure, and that because of my unfortunate family life, no one expected anything different from me.

My aunt would put her arm around me and say things like, "Steve, I know life is hard for you, but no one expects anything good from you after all you have gone through. No one expects you to do well in life after what your parents have done to you." I imagine now that she had the best of intentions, but that was certainly not clear to me then. Her comments only served to infuriate me. In reaction I made more life rules—with the best of intentions!

Incompatible Concepts

Although I was doing a lot of stupid things and my anger was causing some bad consequences, I was convinced I was on the right track. After all, I had made a commitment to myself that I would not be like my dad. I was convinced he had screwed up my life because he had bailed out on us as a family. It never crossed my mind that being angry and doing stupid things, and having good intentions not to be a bad dad like my father, were incompatible concepts.

In spite of the negative situations in my life, I still had good intentions—supported by the life rules and vows I held to make life work the way I wanted it to. I knew what I wanted to do with my life, and I knew what I wanted to become. It was clear to me that my life rules would make life work and prevent problems. The vows about my life rules kept me focused on controlling things, people, situations, or whatever was needed to make my good intentions succeed. The concept of my good intentions was all wrapped up in my life rules and my vows to make them happen.

While I had good intentions, I was still too young to make them work. That would wait until I was in my forties and able to put it all together. But the good intentions were crystal-clear to me at that young age!

Best Intentions

My best intentions after my parents divorced were that I would never let divorce happen to my wife and kids, I would never abandon my children, and I would help them walk through life instead of letting them figure it out on their own.

I committed to succeed at life, to be a great husband and a great dad, to live a balanced life of maturity and wisdom, and to be my own man and do whatever it took to succeed at what was important to me.

The Downslide

My life continued on a horrible downslide after my parents' divorce. I went from a sixth-grade student earning all A's and a few B's to one who received nothing but D's and F's. Then I failed junior high. Ashamed, I started to hate others. Because I was one of the smallest kids in my school, I developed an aggressive attitude to prove to everyone that I was manly.

I constantly did things that got me into a lot of trouble. While I had made life rules that were supposed to be good and helpful, I wasn't experiencing much of anything that was either good or helpful. Rather, I experienced anger, shame, and guilt. I was captivated by whatever feelings triggered a negative reaction to life.

As I look back, it seems odd that while I had made good life rules, my indignation at life meant that I neglected those rules and was heading down the wrong path. Despite my good intentions, I was living my life in a rage. In my mind I could never connect the dots.

Anger Rules

A few years ago my son told me that when he was about nine or ten, he made a life rule. At the time he had been having some problems with his mother. He told himself that he was going to use his anger to protect himself from life events and people who might screw him over. Hearing he chose to use anger as his path hit me between the eyes.

I made life rules about how I would be a great man and a good husband and father, but none of my life rules included using anger. Yes, I went down a path of rage and I used my anger to try to make everything work out. But I never planned it that way. Regardless of my intentions, anger ruled my life and was my biggest problem. I couldn't get past it for almost forty-five years.

Like Father, Like Son

Anger has been one of my great struggles, and it is also one of my son's. He remembers saying he would use anger to solve his problems in life—and he also says he thought he could rid himself of that rage. I hope he can. For more than four decades, I was never able to get rid of mine.

Regardless of my good intentions, because I had been hurt by people and life, my anger ruled me. The fact that I have finally experienced a heart change and a renewal of my good intentions has again put me on the path of loving my son and becoming the dad I had always hoped to be.

Steve White in 2nd grade, in
the year 1960

Steve White and his
young brother Douglas

My mother's photo before
she married my dad

I am standing between my Uncle Dave and Aunt Helen. Aunt Helen is the
tall blond, hot babe lady in the story "Life's Events".
The photo is sometime after I got out of the Navy

CHANGING
PARTNERS

Although I had negative thoughts toward my dad because of the divorce, I also had negative thoughts toward my mother. In short, I was mad at both parents. They each told me bad things about the other, and each wanted me to live with them. The question of who I would chose to live with became an ongoing battle between my parents, and I still do not know what was true about all the stories I heard. Actually, their stories did not faze me. I was so focused on my own needs that I did what I thought was best for me. I thought it best to live with my father, so I moved in with him when I was fourteen—and took my nine-year-old brother with me. This broke my mother's heart. I had no idea of what I was doing and how it would affect her.

Life continued to disintegrate. After I moved in with my dad and stepmom, I began experiencing a whole new set of problems. After about a year, my brother went back to live with our mom. She had promised him a bicycle, and that triggered his decision.

No divorce is good news, and my parents' divorce was a truly bad event for everyone in the family. What are the odds that any of us did what was right? After three years of living with my dad and stepmom, I was in no better a mental or emotional state than before, and I wanted to run away from everyone—and from all of life. So that's what I did.

I signed up to join the Navy, though I couldn't officially enlist until I turned eighteen—which was six months down the road. Still, I made a commitment, and when my eighteenth birthday rolled around, I left my old life behind to start a new one in the military. The boot camp was at the U.S. Naval Station in San Diego, California. The day I officially joined the Navy, my life dropped into the toilet.

The Elevator Event

My first day in the Navy was in Los Angeles at the Naval building for new recruits. We were there to learn all the rules and regulations. Then we were to take a bus to San Diego for the boot camp.

When I got into an elevator to go to the top of the building for our session, there was one other guy in the elevator. When I saw him push the button to the same place I was going, I introduced myself.

He said his name was Richard White.

"That's my dad's name," I said. "What is your middle name?"

"Allan," he said.

I asked how it was spelled, and he told me. "That's my dad's middle name," I said. "Where are you from?" "Providence, Rhode Island."

"That's where I am from," I said. "I was born at the main hospital right in town."

He said he was, too. Then he told me the name of the hospital and the doctor. They were also the same as mine.

I told him my birthday; he was just a couple of months older. Then I then asked him his dad's name.

He didn't know. His mom had sex with a guy who never married her.

I didn't say anything more to him, but I was remembering some bad stories my mom had told me about my dad while they had lived in Providence. As I replayed what I had just heard, I became infuriated. Then we arrived at the room where we were to report for service.

My Recruiter Was an Idiot

The Navy recruiter had promised me that I could pick my job and the location where I would be stationed. That was why I joined the Navy instead of the Marines. At the time, I was in love with a girl named Jenny, who lived in Riverside, California, just a couple of hours from San Diego. I was hoping to marry Jenny, so staying in Southern California was critical to me.

But during this initiation meeting, the first thing the commander said was, "Any and all promises and commitments made prior to today from any recruiters are null and void." He explained that the Navy had no control over what those idiots said to people, and that they were sorry for any issues it caused. My mind exploded. This and the elevator event were a nightmare.

Anger filled me over what that idiot did to me as a recruiter, and over having met someone who could be my half-brother. I wanted to bail out—and the sooner the better. But that could not happen during boot camp.

A few days later I found out that recruits could attend any religious service at any time, and the leaders could not prevent this. So I started going to every one that was held at the chapel. I went to Mormon, Jehovah's Witness, Buddhist, Protestant, Catholic, and whatever other religious services there were. These services happened every day, and for hours I sat there and read cowboy stories by Louis **L'Amour**. Because I was able to get out of so much work, everybody in my squad hated me. But now in life I didn't care about having them like me and I didn't give a _ _ _ _ about what I was doing.

A Nightmare!

Eight weeks into boot camp, I received orders about where I would be stationed and what my job would be. I was going to be an electrician … on a submarine stationed in Florida. It was like the entire Navy command structure had set me up for disaster. First, I was claustrophobic. I knew I couldn't work in a submarine. Second, as a three-year-old, I had been hospitalized after I had stuck my finger in a wall plug. Ever since, at least until my mid-thirties, I was terrified of electricity. And third, the Navy recruiter had promised me I would get stationed at either Long Beach or San Diego, and that I would have my choice of the type of ship and job assignment. After finding out I had been lied to, I considered bailing out of boot camp.

The morning after I received my orders, I went to the commander on base and told him why I was furious. I told him that the things they did to me had to be changed. "If these orders are not changed," I said, "I will be forced to go AWOL."

"I don't give a ---- if you bail out and go AWOL or anything else," he said. "But if you do, you are going to spend your life career in the brig. And there is nothing I can do about your friking orders." His words were nastier.

A Miracle!

I left the building in despair, beyond anger, and hopeless. Terrified about the job in Florida, I knew I could not and would not do it. On the way back to the barracks, a thought came to me. At one of the church services I had heard someone from a Christian organization called Campus Crusade for Christ.

I can't say I paid attention to what he said; I am sure I was instead reading my Louis **L'Amour** book. But I remembered him saying something about coming to a place in our lives where we are willing to admit that what we have been doing is wrong, and that we could turn in faith to Jesus Christ. He said Jesus was God's Son and that he died for our sin, proving God loves us. The Campus Crusade speaker also said that God would reveal himself to us if we are willing to follow him in life—and that if we are not sure we believe in God, we can ask him to reveal or prove himself to us.

I turned around and went to the chapel. Nobody was there. I sat in a chair and wept and admitted to God that I didn't know for sure if I believed in him, but that I had certainly screwed up my life and was sick and tired of living the way I had. I appealed to God: "If you are real, will you prove it to me? Will you change my orders and give me a job on a ship that is doable? If you will, I will follow you for the rest of my life."

I walked out of the chapel feeling like the world had been lifted off my back. On the way to the barracks I saw a pay phone and called my girlfriend. I told her what happened and that I might become a Christian, depending on what happened, and that I had asked God to prove he was real.

About a week later a new set of orders came for me. As far as I know, it was the only set of orders that came into camp at that time. Everyone was shocked—including the commander. I was to be stationed in Long Beach, California, on a big ship called the *Juneau* that was above water. My new job was a machinery repair man. My school for training would be three months long and was located in San Diego!

My advice is not to pray the kind of prayer I did in the chapel unless you are serious. All of this certainly changed my attitude and my thoughts about life. I had some new good intentions and made three more life rules: First, I was going to believe in God and follow Christ. Second, I was going to become a great Christian. Third, I was going to learn a lot about God and help others get to know him. These three life rules became experiences over time because of real life changes!

Opposite Ends of a Spectrum

I felt a change happening in my life that was real, and during that first year in the Navy I was really happy. I got stationed where I wanted to be in Southern California, near my home, and I was able to continue hanging out with my friends. I also made a new set of friends who were Christians. I stayed in the area for about a year and a half before traveling in the ship all over the Far East. Because of the change the Navy made with my job and location, I assumed things would continue working out the way I expected and that everything would be great. But that is not the way things happened.

In my first year and a half I learned a lot about Christianity from Bible study and reading Christian books. In my mind, everything about me and my faith was settled. But life's events were still going wrong, and my head started getting screwed up. I thought I had become a spiritual hero, but without my realizing it, I was becoming a classically arrogant and overbearing religious zealot. My Christianity was becoming more of an intellectual concept instead of a personal faith connecting deeper with God and experiencing an abundant spiritual life. Though I had connected with God at first, and even experienced a miracle, I still had some wrong expectations about how life was to work out and how people should act toward me. I thought I could control events and outcomes, but now I was learning otherwise.

I started slipping backward in attitude and behavior. Although I was still a believer, I was not following Christ's character. That personal, internal change I had experienced seemed to have evaporated. I was not on track, and once again I was getting angry about life because of all the junk still going wrong. I had head knowledge of God and Jesus, but my heart knowledge was lacking. I thought being a Christian would keep me from experiencing my old patterns of life, which was something I missed. And I thought being a Christian meant that people would treat me the way I wanted and expected them to.

I lived in two places at opposite ends of a spectrum. On the one hand I wanted to be spiritual, but on the other I was full of anger. When it came to fixing things and people, the angry side won out. Anger had again become a habitual, major part of my makeup.

In my time in the Navy, a number of bad things happened with superiors I worked for, and those triggered three more life rules and vows: First, I will not be like them if and when I become a leader. Second, I will not trust people in leadership positions if they act arrogantly. And third, at all times and at all costs I will protect myself from them.

I hated these military leaders for what they did to those under their command. We were treated in some very foul ways. Their lying and overly opinionated attitudes were two key factors that set me off against them. While I tried to make life work while in the Navy, I wound up hating it and I could not wait to get out.

This is the ship I was on during my career in the Navy and
went to Vietnam on it. I also have a picture of me
sitting on it on the way to Vietnam

Two Deaths Caused Insight

Although I was in the Navy, I was still staying in touch and
hanging out with two Christian friends who were not in the service.
At some point in the second year my best friend, Bill Telliard, lost
his wife to cancer, and my newer friend, Mike Gemme, who was my
Christian mentor, lost his wife to leukemia. We were all in our early
twenties. The death of their wives broke my heart. Their experiences
went well beyond any disaster in my life, and the way they handled
them showed how spiritually mature they were.

For months I observed how Bill and Mike walked through
this cloud of darkness with very different attitudes than my own.
Fortunately, it opened me up to hearing some things from Mike about
my Christian lifestyle. He told me that during his wife's sickness and
right after her death, he was uncomfortable hanging out with me.

One day, while driving with him in my car, Mike said I was a
completely arrogant and off-base Christian. He used some strong,
colorful words to describe me and my Christian walk. He called me a
"human lawn mower" and said he had been praying that something
terrible would happen to me—like getting my arms cut off—so I would

be open to learn from God. He didn't hesitate to give me the specifics of what was wrong with me: I was cocky, talked too much, and was not at all like the person God desired a Christian to be.

Looking back on it, I'm surprised that I was thankful for what Mike unloaded on me, and I knew that what he said was true. It made sense. Though he was agitated when he said them, I realized that what he said was very important. I was actually grateful to God for revealing some things about myself through someone else. Mike was right, I was a complete spiritual jerk. I was surprised that I was happy to believe it about myself. Instead of feeling angry at him, I was thankful.

I thought about that experience for months, and Mike and I spent a lot of time together. I was growing again, and our friendship was back on track.

Stuck in the Mud

Although some clear insights came to me, and I was glad to have seen them, I made some more wrong assumptions about how life and other Christians generally should be, and how I was now better than others. It was the same old arrogance that I had not mastered. On that topic, I was stuck in the mud. I thought that what I learned made me a new person, but I didn't realize that knowing something intellectually does not guarantee life changes. Eventually I wound up living in another negative pattern for a couple of years.

What do I mean by wrong assumptions? I judged other Christians as being screwed up based on what they did wrong. Somehow I didn't realize I had done the same things. I developed a bad attitude toward Christians, particularly Christian leaders. They were not like me, so they came up wanting. I thought I was smarter than others because I had learned about my faults and assumed that my faults were now fixed. I judged others as stupid. I spent a lot of time thinking about and then telling people about their faults. When they reacted negatively, this confirmed my judgment of them, and so I went further down the road. I was clueless that I was clueless.

My best friend when I was in high school, Bill Telliard. His wife had died in her 20s and his kids are those that called me Uncle Steve

My first time I was on the naval ship called the Juneau, heading to Vietnam

My other best friend Mike Gemme, and one of
my mentors. His wife had died in her 20s also

MORE RULES AND
VOWS

When I got out of military service in 1974 I felt totally rejected by American society, as did most of us who returned from Vietnam. Americans had been very negative about our country stepping into other nations' problems. Reports on TV and in newspapers constantly complained about Americans having to fight for the Vietnamese. The weird thing was, the people in our country were mad at us who had no choice about being in the war. At age eighteen, if we were not in college, we were being mandated to join the military.

The attitude in this country was very negative toward anything that came close to being military. I couldn't find a decent job because no one wanted to hire Vietnam veterans. I wound up working as a dishwasher at a café called Patty Ann's. It was owned by a couple I had worked for while I was in high school. Back then they managed a steakhouse called Squires in Riverside, California. Ron and Patty Sesler hired me, even though I had been in Vietnam, because they were good friends. They were like parents to me. In January 2009, after forty years, I met them again at a restaurant they now own in Seal Beach, California, called Patty's Place. One of the best in Orange County!

I worked for them at Patty Ann's Café for a short time, but I grew frustrated at being a dishwasher and not being able to find a job I wanted. So I moved to Yuma, Arizona, and lived with my mom and stepdad, who was willing to let me work for him as an appliance repairman. This allowed me to get reconnected to my mom after becoming a Christian. I appreciated that they were willing to let me work for them, but the real reason I wound up in Yuma was that I had a hard time with society's attitude against Vietnam vets. Because of that, I felt forced to move to a place I didn't really want to live. I hated hot weather, and that is about all you get in Yuma. I kept paying rent at my place in Riverside, California, hoping to come back to my home as soon as possible.

I got into the appliance repair work and enjoyed the job because I was making money, and it had the potential to give me enough to keep paying my rent. I didn't have any friends in Yuma, but my younger brother lived with my mom, so we were together again.

But another downside about living in Yuma—other than heat—was that I felt my mom was making me go to her church, which I disliked because of their rules about communion and other specific denominational do's and don'ts. I didn't think the preaching helped me walk through my life, because it was directed at a much older crowd. Every Sunday seemed like a wasted day.

I wanted to go to church, but I wanted to go to one I liked. I felt I had no option about going somewhere else, however, because I thought Mom wanted me at her church and that she would be embarrassed if I went somewhere else. While she had good intentions, I felt she was controlling me. I was irritated that once again someone else was controlling my life. It felt like being back in the Navy.

While living in Yuma, I made more life rules and vows: First, I won't live with parents again. Second, I won't belong to any denomination, but will go to a nondenominational church. And third, I won't act or sound like religious people.

Home Again and Gone Again

After six months in Arizona, I moved back to my home in Riverside. I again started hanging out with my friend Mike Gemme and gained more insights about myself. It started dawning on me that I had created some of my own problems because of my thoughts, attitudes, and decisions.

I realized that some people in my life were treating me the way they did because I had made them think I wanted to be helped. So they were trying to fix me. These were people I went to church with or had weekly Bible study meetings with. A lot of people tried to make me look like the typical Christian, which involved following a list of do's and don'ts. Some people at church were offering up their religious rules and constantly giving me their opinions about what I should and shouldn't do. This frustrated me because I didn't agree with their opinions. I wanted to leave this pattern of life behind and start anew.

I don't remember all the details of this event, but it became obvious to me that I had screwed up so badly and had negatively impacted so many people, I had to do something dramatic to change it all. So around midnight I moved out of the house I was renting and left the county. Without telling anyone, I packed everything in my car and left.

I had made arrangements to rent a cabin in the mountains in Crestline, California. I had also gotten a job as a mechanic at a gas station. So I left when no one in my neighborhood or at church would know. I didn't want anyone, including my parents, to know where I would be living. I chose not to install a phone line at the new cabin. (That was before cell phones.) I didn't want to talk to people who knew me, and I didn't want them to know how to reach me. I was going to change my lifestyle and my attitudes—and not allow the people I knew to tell me what I needed to do with my life. For almost a year I never talked to my mom, dad, or stepmom. But I did let my two best friends, Mike Gemme and Bill Telliard, know where I lived, and I stayed in touch with them.

In this way I started living a new life. I went to a really great church in San Bernardino that Bill Telliard was attending, and the pastor was very different from all the others I had met. I really loved the church. My friend Mike Gemme was going to Charles Swindoll's church, and I started reading his books. At times I also went to his church. His books and the teaching I received at both churches provided a lot of insight and fueled my desire to keep on a new and better path.

A BLIND DATE CAUSED A MARRIAGE, AND MARRIAGE CAUSED BLINDNESS

While living in the mountains of California I went from being an auto mechanic to becoming the assistant manager of a supermarket. A few years later I got into real estate and became very successful. I made a lot of money and owned six homes. One of my houses was in Lake Arrowhead, where I was living with a friend, Steve Waller, who owned a sports shop in San Bernardino called Sports Country.

I had started snow skiing a lot, and as a weekend hobby I became a ski patrolman, then a ski instructor. Because of all my skiing, Steve Waller started using me as a demo skier for his sports shop's products. I got to wear the best ski suits and used the best skis. I was having a good time skiing, and I loved what I did in real estate.

At some point early in 1981, when I was twenty-eight, I went on a blind date. That date eventually led to my marriage on November 15, 1981. I knew I needed to get serious to achieve my "best intentions" about being a great husband.

But that plan never got off the ground. It started falling apart the day after our wedding. We had a knock-down, drag-out argument, and things spiraled downward from there. A few days before our marriage, Deb said that she was certain I could not love her the way she needed to be loved. I told her to trust me, and I really thought I could meet her expectations. I certainly wanted to, but again I was clueless. I didn't have what it would take, and I didn't know it.

When I talk about my life problems, I know I am pretty accurate. I have documented my life's stories in journals from the beginning of my marriage up to today. As I experienced events, I wrote them down. Looking at my journal, clear patterns of negative consequences started showing up. For the first four years of my marriage, I hardened myself against the reality of those bad patterns. I explained them away and denied the failures, assuming that if I kept controlling people or situations, it would all work out. I usually just blamed others for my problems. Or I blamed life. I never connected the symptoms and consequences to my root issues. Trying to control circumstances and people was a routine event. I was blind to the real reasons things were going wrong, and I was ignorant to what I did and did not have control over.

I Don't Need No Stinking Agreement!

One of the first things my wife and I fought over was whether she would be a stay-at-home mom. I wanted this, but she did not. I saw it as a requirement for someone to be a great mom to her kids. We had discussed this before our marriage, and I thought we had an agreement. But now that we were married, my wife found herself bored to tears and feeling insecure about my income, because in real estate sales I worked on a straight commission. She wanted to go to work to make sure we were financially secure.

This argument went on for some time—actually, during our entire marriage. In my mind I always won the arguments because I was standing on my good intentions. To relent to her desires would put my kids at risk—as I had been at risk as a kid by not having my parents around. That was not going to happen! To paraphrase a line from *The Treasure of the Sierra Madre*, I didn't need no stinking agreement to make things work out!

My wife started feeling that I couldn't be reasoned with. She probably felt she needed to convince me I was being a failure, hoping that would change my mind. So she became very critical about me and my work. Because the first big concept we argued about was work, it became increasingly difficult for us to cooperate on anything. Far from working together, we were working against each other—and hoping the other would give in.

We had two children. In our first year of marriage we had a son we named Ian, then two years later we had our daughter, Kari. From my point of view back then, my perspective was always the correct one. I see now that I should have handled things differently.

In hindsight I see that I wasn't inclined to discover her needs first; I considered only my own. And because I was determined to be the best husband I could possibly be, that meant my wife would not work outside the home. It never occurred to me that being the best husband would mean putting my wife's needs and concerns ahead of mine. I genuinely meant well, and I thought I was on the right track. But I was wrong.

My motive for Deb to stay home came from the fact that when I was a child, my mother was always at work and my father did not live with us. I would do things in a different and better way. The life rule I developed out of this was that I would not let my kids grow up without a parent who was around regularly.

Moving Didn't Fix the Problems

Our house in the mountains of Lake Arrowhead was beautiful and large, with a lake view and only a few neighbors. My wife, however, grew up in a city living close to all her family and friends. When she got married she moved from a city environment to the mountains of Southern California—with no friends or family nearby. We had a great house with good neighbors, which did make her comfortable. And we were only about forty-five minutes away from her family, so it was acceptable to her. But I had made it clear before we got married that I wanted to move to the mountains in either Montana or Colorado, and she agreed to this plan.

After getting married, we went on a vacation to a few mountain states and toured the areas to see where we wanted to live. Within a year after finding a home in Colorado, we moved.

Snakes and Cows Were Neighbors

We decided Western Colorado was the place to live, so we moved into a six-hundred square-foot log cabin on forty acres out in the country at the base of the Grand Mesa. It was an hour and a half drive to the nearest real city. This meant a very different style of life compared to living near neighbors who were friends, and having family reunions weekly. We had a couple of neighbors who were elderly, and they lived a half-mile away. I liked the place very much. My wife had a different view.

The day we moved in she found a five-foot bull snake on top of one of the boxes she was unpacking. She freaked out. The second day we awoke to cows all over our porch and yard. She freaked out again. Colorado is an open-range state, which means you do not have to have fences to keep your cows on your own property.

During the first week while I was at work, my wife had a meltdown. I worked in the city of Grand Junction, an hour and a half drive from the ranch house we were renting. I was a new sales person in a newly bought water-treatment company. I thought it was just a temporary job. I was planning to get back into real estate soon. For my wife, the snake and cows did not equal a family reunion; she had no friends, no family, and a husband she could not control. She went to one of our neighbors, and they called me at work to say they thought my wife was having an emotional breakdown.

Heaven Versus Hell

How this panned out will come as no surprise. My intentions were good, but I forced the situation to achieve them. Basically, I expected Deb to shape up and get on board with the new lifestyle. We were going to enjoy this new life—come hell or high water! And though this was heaven for me, hell did come—at least for her.

Now as I am able to look back with clarity, the consequences of my decision to move to rural Colorado were fairly awful. She must have felt extremely insecure and lonely. It was probably becoming clear to her that she wasn't going to convince me to move back to California. From there, things continued going downhill. It is sad and ironic now to see that my intention to be a great father and provider negated my intention to be a great husband.

Things got bad fast. My wife attacked me and accused me of doing things the wrong way. I repeatedly ignored, justified, excused, and defended myself. But she needed the chance to vent. I always thought that when she finally understood my good intentions, she would come around from her negative reactions and support my wisdom. The fact that she accused me and attacked me with anger made me think she must be stupid. After all, I knew what I was doing and why I was doing things. But even when I told her my reasons, she was never able to buy into my perspectives and plans.

Real insight came to me many years later, and I understood what had gone wrong. My wife felt trapped. She needed her desires fulfilled just like I did, but I was the macho man in control of where we were going to live. And she knew I was not moving back to California. She felt trapped in a foreign place, surrounded by nothing familiar. Had I known then what I know now, I would have realized things were going very wrong, instead of thinking they would work themselves out.

I could have listened and reflected on the things she discussed to make sure I knew what she was saying—and she knew I was listening. I could have asked questions about her needs and motives. I could have put her needs ahead of mine and maybe earned some respect. I would do those things now, but then I did none of them. Instead, I focused on controlling life and others, thinking I could make it all work out for the good. Without realizing it, I was using people to fill my personal needs of being loved, having self-worth, feeling significant, and living in security. I was missing a better way of doing what my heart desired.

I didn't need to be perfect to be loved by my children or my wife, but my limited perspective caused some real problems in our marriage. I wish I had learned about my problems a lot sooner. Fortunately, I started questioning my preconceptions to see what was wrong and how things could be changed.

My good intention was to raise my kids in an environment that would be best for them. I wanted to get my family out of Southern California, which I did not consider a good place to raise children. It was too busy, too materialistic, and had too many drugs and druggies. I wanted to benefit my family by living in real mountains. Our California mountains were not big enough or beautiful enough for the kind of skiing, hiking, and camping I loved. The life rule that developed from this was that in moving the family to Western Colorado, I would be the best dad I could and raise my kids in the best environment possible.

Through all of this I had good intentions, but again I was blinded by them. What helped reveal that I was on a wrong path?

THE UGLY, BAD AND GOOD

One of my goals was to prove to myself and the world that I had what it took to succeed, make life work, and enjoy life. But it became clear at that time that the world did not really care about me or my goals. Although I believed in God and thought I was on the right path, because of my anger, bitterness, and resentment toward life and everyone around me, my trajectory was heading into a wall of failure. Until then, I had been unaware of that trajectory. But I started to realize my lifestyle was *ugly*.

I had good intentions, and I thought my opinions and plans were based on wisdom. There probably was some wisdom to them, but I couldn't make everything work out the way I intended because until my mid-forties, I was committed to the life rules and vows I had previously made. That was *bad*.

Lots of good things happened in my life. Because of my personality, I was typically happy, at least I thought I was. I enjoyed life, but when I started to realize that I had been repeating negative thoughts over and over about certain people and events, those thoughts hooked me and held me hostage to my anger. Realizing that, I started on a path to find insights for change. That was *good*.

SECTION 2

INSIGHTS FOR CHANGE

The following stories tell of things that provided insight about what was causing the failures in my life. They made me realize I really had problems, and that I needed to make a commitment for change. I became aware of what abilities I could control that would influence me in the right direction.

A DISNEYLAND
VACATION

While living in Colorado we took a week vacation to Disneyland. I grew up in Garden Grove, California, and went to Disneyland all the time as a kid. My grandmother lived three blocks from the park, and I could ride my bicycle to her house and then walk to Disneyland. Over the years I went there well over a hundred times. Back then they did not charge people to get in—you just had to pay for each ride you went on. So I loved going there. And I convinced my family we ought to go and spend a week on vacation. My son was ten and my daughter was eight, and it was their first time at Disneyland.

We stayed at a hotel across from Disneyland. In the mornings I hung out at the pool and read books and wrote in my journal. Deb and the kids did what they wanted in the mornings, and after lunch we walked across the street and spent the rest of the day at Disneyland.

On our second day, while the family was up in our hotel room, I was sitting at the pool reading a book about marriage and enjoying the sun. I had my journal to make notes about insights while pondering all the dilemmas in our marriage. It seemed that everything was wrong between us. I was pretty confident that the book I was reading would help, so I was very focused on reading and thinking about all of our issues and what might bring about some changes.

A Voice from Heaven

While sitting in a lounge chair sunbathing and reading, I thought someone spoke to me. The comment I heard was, "Put the book down and watch." I looked around and wondered who said that. I didn't see anyone, so I kept reading. Then I heard it again. I felt a bit odd that I didn't see anyone talking to me, and I was starting to wonder what was going on. But I kept reading.

A minute later I heard the same comment for a third time. This time it was loud and clear. I put the book down, looked around, and tried to figure out how I could be hearing something that clearly when no one was talking to me. Then I realized this had to be God's Spirit speaking. Maybe it was inwardly in my mind and not audible. I don't know. I do know this was something I had never experienced. It seemed obvious that something was about to happen and I was going to observe or experience it.

There were fewer than ten people in the pool. Within seconds, two kids in the water came up to the side of the pool next to where I was sitting. I was about ten feet away. As I listened to them talking, it was clear they were brothers. One was probably ten or twelve, and the younger one was probably about six or eight years old.

A Chicken in the Pool

The older brother was trying to get the younger one to let go of the side and go into the deeper water. The younger brother would not let go of the side, so the older one started splashing water in his face. He kept shoving water into the kid's face and telling him he was a chicken. Every time the young one turned toward the older one, he would get water splashed into his face. He started crying and telling his brother to stop it. I started to get really mad.

The older one kept calling his brother names and kept splashing him in the face. I started looking around for the parents. I was going to get them to do something, but they were not at the pool. The older one grabbed the younger one and pulled him away from the side of the pool. The young one started screaming, but this only made his brother start spitting water into his face. I got so irritated, I almost jumped into the water to drag the older one out of the pool.

Then I heard another comment: "Just watch." This problem continued for another couple of minutes. I couldn't believe what a fool this brother was, and I was thinking about pounding him. The older one kept pulling his little brother by the feet backwards into the deep end of the pool. The young one was screaming and choking as he was being pulled. I was in a panic. I felt like I needed to do something, but I had clearly heard, "Just watch." The kid was screaming so loudly, the older one finally let him go, and he swam to the steps and ran off.

Learning to Swim

A minute later, two other brothers came to the pool and stopped in front of me. They were talking about going swimming. The older one had on a long bathrobe and a pair of leather strapped sandals. The younger one was barefoot and wore just a swimsuit. He was holding his older brother's hand.

They looked about the same age as the other two kids. The younger one wanted to learn how to swim but was a bit nervous—and told his brother that. Then they started talking about the younger one's learning how to swim. The young one said to his older brother, "Will you please help me and not scare me?" The older kid was very calm and encouraged his brother to let him help him. He said he could trust him to be very careful and that they had all day to learn.

The older brother took off his robe and sandals, held his brother's hand, and walked him into the pool. As they got to the last step, the older boy held his brother against his chest and walked around with him for a while in the shallow end.

The older brother asked the younger one if he would let him hold his body and teach him to float. It took a few minutes, but he finally agreed. So the older one walked around the shallow end holding his brother horizontally while letting him pretend he was swimming. He did it for a long time.

Then he taught him how to hold his breath and float. He stood right next to him while letting him try. After about a half hour in the water, the younger one was ready to get out. He asked his brother if they could stop. The older one said yes, and he carried his younger brother out of the water, holding his hands while walking up the steps. When they got out of the pool, the younger one said he was chilly. The older brother took a towel and dried his brother off, put his robe around him, and sat him down and put his own sandals on his brother. Then he took his hand and they left.

A Swamp with Alligators

While I watched these four boys, God spoke to me in a very gracious way. He told me that the way I had been trying to fix my marriage and teach my wife how to be a better wife and Christian was like the guy I had seen dragging his brother backwards into the deep end of the pool. "Debbie has made it clear that she is afraid of whatever is in the deep end of her life," he said, "and you are dragging her backwards into a terrifying place. She feels like there are alligators in the deep end, and you are dragging her by the feet backwards into a swamp. She doesn't know how to live the way you want her to live, and you are causing the same things in her as that older brother was causing in his younger brother's life."

I kept thinking about the other brother who had loved and cared for his younger brother, and was doing it just like Jesus would have done. God made it clear that this event was for me to experience what I had been like—and how I needed to change and love and care for Deb. As I thought about the robe and the sandals one of the boys wore, I envisioned Jesus and the way he so loved the world.

God Unfolded Things for Me

As I pondered how I had been treating my wife, I felt I fell somewhere between the rude older brother and the gentle, patient older brother. On the one hand I was trying to help my wife, but on the other hand I was truly dragging her into a fearful place. I knew I had not been patient and loving like that gracious older brother. I was expecting her to toe the line and follow my suggestions and expectations—it was like dragging her backwards into a deep swamp with alligators. I realized that a lot of the things that happened in Debbie's past terrified her, and the way I had been doing things was making it worse. I was distressed at how I had been lording it over her, and yet I was so glad that God had graciously revealed things to me without making me feel ridiculed.

You may question whether this message I heard was direct from God's Spirit. But I can assure you that I believe it was. At the time I certainly didn't have the insights, thoughts, and wisdom to put those things together. It was so far beyond my ability to see the lesson and learn from it, that for me it was a no-brainer to see this whole episode was from God's Spirit. I couldn't make this stuff up. I sat there and wrote about it in my journal, crying in delight that God had shown me this!

I spent that day delighting in the insights God had shown me, and I never mentioned it to my wife. It wasn't because I was afraid of admitting it, but I wanted her to experience a real change in me and not just hear about the intellectual concepts I experienced while sitting at the pool. I realized how far off track I had been—and that God loved me and Debbie enough to provide such a vacation.

The more I thought it over in the following days, the more clearly I realized that my priority had been on fixing my wife and not myself. I was trying to control her and was more concerned about her meeting my needs than I was about being patient, gracious, and loving toward her.

As each day unfolded that week, I learned more and more about how I had been reacting in the wrong way to my wife. I almost got mad at myself, except that I remembered how gracious God had been in showing me these things. New desires and priorities began occurring to me, and I knew I needed to change inwardly—and to stay open and connected at deeper levels with God to bring about those internal changes.

PICTURES WORTH A THOUSAND WORDS

In our home we had a hallway lined with pictures of our family. The kids appeared in photos taken over a ten-year period. For years, I walked by those photos and couldn't help but smile. It felt good as I looked at them and thought of how wonderful my kids were. It didn't matter how bad a mood I might have been in; every time I looked at those photos, I felt really good and enjoyed positive memories about life with my kids.

During this time in our lives, my son had become involved with drugs. I was particularly brokenhearted one day when I realized he was probably addicted. He had been living a lie for a long time, and it all hit the fan one week. As I stopped in front of my favorite photo of my son, I began smiling and became engrossed with the picture. I was filled with joy at how wonderful my son was and how much I loved him.

I never suspected that my son could have been involved in drugs. Then I experienced God saying that he sees me like I see my son. I broke down in tears and felt the true love of God surround me. I could not separate myself from God's love or his view of my worth as his creation.

I wanted to be the same way toward my son, no matter what he did wrong. I didn't want him to separate himself from my love and my vision of his value and worth. Remembering this helped me walk through the negative things that were to happen between me and my son (more about this later).

It would be tempting to try to fix him and right all that was going wrong in his life, but this experience in front of my son's picture convinced me to focus on loving rather than rescuing him. The following story shows that my perspectives were changing.

This is the picture of Ian that brought insights about how
God loved me

WINNING AMERICA'S FUNNIEST HOME VIDEO

A few months after this, an accident happened at our home. At the time our son was almost fifteen. Debbie and I were out on a date for our wedding anniversary and had just ordered dinner at a restaurant when my pager went off. I had never used a pager before that day. My company wanted me to carry one, and I told my kids not to call unless it was an emergency. With a sick feeling in my stomach, I went to the lobby and called home.

We were at a popular restaurant called the Red Lobster at the mall in Grand Junction, Colorado. The pay phone was in the middle of the lobby, which was filled with people, so this meant that everyone around me heard most of this phone call. Had it been on video, I might have won $10,000 from *America's Funniest Home Videos*.

The restaurant was about an hour and a half from home, so it wouldn't have been easy to drive home and resolve the problem. I had to call. When I did, the phone rang and rang. I got very nervous.

After thirty or more rings someone finally answered, but it wasn't either of my kids. When I asked who it was, the person hung up. I got fearful, then mad, and I called back again.

This time the phone rang about four times and the same person answered. I demanded to know who it was, and he yelled over to my son, "Hey, it's your dad. What do I tell him?" The person put the phone down without saying anything more and left it on a table.

When my son finally came to the phone, I could tell by his voice that something was very wrong.

I asked what happened. Ian said in a trembling voice, "Dad, I did something really, really bad."

This filled me with panic. I asked him if he was all right—and the whole lobby fell silent!

"I think so," he said.

I asked about his sister Kari, and he told me she was fine and that she was not at home.

My son's voice was a broken whisper when he told me what happened. "When the neighbor heard it and came over, he told me not to say anything to you," Ian said. "He said he would think of something to help me out. So I got afraid and came in and called you. Well ... uh ... I needed to move the car out of the garage for something, and ... well, when I put it back in, I kind of ran the car through the house. It's really bad—really, really bad!"

I asked him exactly how bad it was. "It's really bad, Dad," he said. "I really screwed up bad. I will sell my Nintendo and pay to have it fixed." He said the house was pretty much destroyed, but that at least it was still standing. He had managed to back the car out of the house, and he said the neighbor told him the house itself seemed safe enough to be in. "I called as soon as he told me not to, Dad," Ian said.

To me, that was a very wise and mature thing to do, and I told Ian that.

He repeated how bad it was, and I told him not to worry about it right now. "Who answered the phone?" I asked.

"It was Eddie."

"Why was Eddie there?"

"He was with me when I had to pull the car out of the garage," Ian said. I was confused. "Ian, you don't even know how to drive. Why did you pull the car out of the garage?"

"I had to, Dad. My hacky sack was under the car."

"You pulled the car out of the garage to get the hacky sack? Ian, you really did it to show off, didn't you?"

He admitted that was true.

I asked if he had thrown up. He said almost—and why did I ask that?

I didn't answer, but was about to laugh. I asked if Eddie was OK. He said Eddie had run out of the garage—running home and screaming he didn't do it.

I was now laughing.

He said he was going to bed because he was too tired to stay awake.

I told Ian I loved him, that we would resolve this later, and that he was already forgiven.

When I hung up the phone to go back to the table, everyone in the lobby was looking at me. Some were teary-eyed and some were laughing, but it must have been a great show for all.

I felt so bad for Ian because he had beaten himself up emotionally. There was nothing I could do to punish him that could teach him a better lesson than what he was already learning.

When I got back to the table, I told Debbie the story. I told her that Ian had done something and had punished himself already, and that I wasn't sure we were going to be able to do much more to him. I told her I was very proud that he had called me even after the neighbor had told him not to. She was full of compassion for Ian, but we decided to finish our anniversary dinner before going home.

We had planned to go to the movies after dinner, but I suggested we take the money and buy Ian a gift instead. Deb thought that was great. She suggested we buy a pair of pants Ian wanted. We couldn't wait to get home and see the look on his face when he got a gift instead of punishment.

When we got home, the damage to the house and car was obvious. He had driven the car through the corner of the garage and taken out the support beam to the roof. My main concern was that the roof would collapse. He had missed the gas meter by two inches. The damage was extensive.

In the middle of the garage floor sat a fifteen-pound sledge hammer Ian had used to try straightening out the damage. I laughed out loud at the picture of a kid trying to repair a destroyed house with a sledge hammer. There must have been $10,000 in damage.

It took a strong shaking to wake a groggy Ian, who couldn't even stay awake for the first few minutes. His emotions had gotten the better of him, and we knew we were doing the right thing not to punish him.

We gave him the box with the gift.

A bewildered look came over him. He opened the box and saw the pants he wanted so badly. He could not believe that not only was he not getting punished, but that he had instead received a gift of something he thought he would never get.

I cried as I saw how much this touched him. I could see in his face that this gift had given him a picture of how much we cared for him and how real our love was. I knew we had made a permanent impression that he would remember over the years. I was thankful that my garage got ruined in the way it did because it allowed us the opportunity to show Ian how much we loved him.

The garage got fixed, and our insurance paid for the whole thing. There is a promise in the Bible that says, "We know that in all things God works for the good of those who love him, who have been called according to his purpose" (Rom. 8:28).

Before, I would never have reacted to my son's misadventures the way I did. I think it shows that my attitudes were changing and I was starting to respond to things in a better way. Remembering my son's story helped me stay on the right track. It takes focusing on the good. But remembering that the good can overcome the bad is always helpful—and this includes remembering even horrible things, such as in the following story.

The Duffel Bag

A year after standing in the hallway looking at the family pictures, I found myself going through my son's duffel bag in the trunk of his car after he had been arrested again for drugs. (The car was the one he had crashed into the house. We had given him that car on his sixteenth birthday.) I was looking for dope in the duffel bag, and I was sure I would find it. Ian had run away with another drug addict, and finally they got busted. I was furious about the whole event. Now I was rifling through the bag determined to find the proof of his guilt. I was a man with a mission who knew his son had a terrible problem.

I found a wallet in the bag and was sure it would contain incriminating evidence. I opened it, but there was nothing except a photo of my son when he was younger. It was my favorite photo, the same one I'd seen in the hallway a year earlier when I heard from God. I broke down and sobbed.

I didn't care at that point if I found all kinds of drugs in the bag. I loved my son. I knew he was guilty of drug possession and use, and I didn't need to prove anything. Actually, I didn't even care about his guilt; I loved him and that's all that mattered. The law would do whatever it would, and I didn't need to add anything to his punishment or guilt. I wanted Ian to feel mercy from me, but I also wanted him to understand his value and worth—not only to his family, but also to God. How could I not want this? I remembered what God had said to me in the hallway a year earlier. "This is how I see you and love you, Steve."

After finding Ian's wallet, I had a surprising reaction. I started to understand how we are all capable of doing things that ruin our lives. I saw that my own pattern of anger at my son was similar to his drug abuse. That surprised me.

All I wanted to do was to love my son—instead of always thinking I could fix him or correct the things he did wrong. Yes, he had problems, but why dwell on the negative? I realized I had the same ability to control my remembering the positive things I had learned as I did the negative. That picture of my son is still on the hallway and in his wallet, and I don't ever want to forget how loved he is.

Over time, this concept of remembering the positives and not focusing on the negatives has made a huge difference in my life. I have learned to control what I choose to think about. Believe me, that is much better than focusing on what others should or should not do.

Being Clueless That I Was Clueless

Because I wanted to experience change after my wife and kids told me I was a "macho, know-it-all jerk," I also started to touch base regularly with a pastor and counselor I knew, Doug Self. Our conversations triggered new questions in my mind, because instead of just telling me what to do, he reflected what I said, exactly the way I said it. He didn't tell me all the should's and shouldn'ts I expected to hear when counselors try to fix people. I started hearing what I was saying, and the way I would say things.

My counseling with Doug revealed some seriously messed-up attitudes and expectations. It planted new seeds for change. Maybe the most important thing I learned was that I was clueless that I was clueless.

The changes started within me. I had a lot of help, using my pastor and several authors as mentors. I was reading books by authors such as Larry Crabb, Watchman Nee, Chuck Swindoll, Greg Boyd, and John Eldredge. I also studied the Bible regularly for insights about myself and others.

In previous years I had used Scripture to justify a lot of my preconceived notions instead of letting the Word expose them. Becoming open to God's perspective and the perspectives of Christian authors helped me become a little less clueless. The concept runs throughout the Bible about God being with us and loving us. This became very real to me. The best part was improving my relationship with God—being connected to him and having faith.

Many men have a big problem with lust. For me, the big problem was anger. I was too angry to bother with lust. Because I wanted to be connected to God, I started winning some of my fights against anger. My old patterns with anger could still bring about bad events, but change was happening.

Over time I also discovered my critical need to remain open and committed to deeper insights and deeper changes. I did not realize at first how easily I could go back to my old patterns. I had experienced God's love, but remembering it daily was one of my hardest struggles.

SECTION 3

SOLUTIONS CAN STILL BE THE ENEMY

BLINDED BY GOOD INTENTIONS

Good thoughts and good plans can go down a wrong path. I had gained new insights about my good intentions, and I experienced some genuine changes in my thoughts and attitudes. I was committed to using them to solve my problems and the problems of the world around me.

Yet I was still blinded by my good intentions because I used more energy and put more pressure on myself and others to make those goals successful. After all, I thought, good intentions are good, and it just seemed right that the world should benefit from what I'd learned. That may have been true had I been on the right path—but I wasn't.

When my good intentions fell apart, I assumed the reason had to do with everyone else's problems and not my own. Eventually I realized I needed a deeper discovery about why some things were still not working to the good. My most important discovery was that I should be caring for my own problems—not the problems of others. This concerns motives, and what I discovered were wrong with mine.

A New Car

My wife wanted and needed a car. I wanted to get her a good one. That was a good intention, but my motives were to save money and be the one to make the final decision. I would know how to provide the best solution to her need, because I am a man who knows a lot about cars. I was confident I would come to the right decision, and that she would be very impressed with my solutions.

But Deb already had a good idea of the type of car she wanted, a Toyota Camry. She wanted one because they had a great reputation for providing comfort and security. She told me the specific equipment she needed in the car, the two most important being an air-conditioner and a cassette tape player. (This was way before cars offered CD players.) My thought was that those were easy things for me to provide. I knew the rest of the stuff was basic to all new cars. What I minimized was her priority for comfort and security.

I thought that because I knew more about cars than she did, I could provide a better solution to what she needed by choosing a different car than the one she wanted. I assumed my decision would be best for her. I should be the one to make the final decision because, after all, I am a man and I know what technical things women need. I would be very smart about making the right buying decision.

To me, all of this seemed like a positive attitude. Well, that was my clueless opinion, and it did not match Deb's idea of the car she wanted to drive to make her feel comfortable and secure.

In the New Testament book of James, there is a description of how wisdom comes from heaven: "But the wisdom that comes from heaven is first of all pure; then peace-loving, considerate, submissive, full of mercy and good fruit, impartial and sincere" (3:17). Nothing I decided about the car fit this description.

Ignoring a Stepdad

I told my wife what I thought she needed and that I would take care of things. I decided to contact my stepfather because my mother had said he was going to sell one of his cars. When I called him, he told me very quickly that I should not buy a car from him. I asked him why. He said he was not comfortable with me having this car. I assumed he was just being nervous about someone in the family having a car he had owned. If it developed mechanical problems, that could cause some bad blood. So I ignored what he said and told him I would call him back and let him know if I would or wouldn't buy his car.

Low Mileage, Cheap Price

Before I contacted him about his car, my stepfather was trying to sell it on the basis of its low mileage and a cheap price. He neglected to tell me why he was selling so cheaply, and I didn't ask. Before talking to Deb about it, I decided to buy it—because it was cheap and had low mileage. I thought that buying the car would make me look wise. I knew my wife wanted a Camry, but I also knew the price tag on one. I wanted to save money, and my stepdad's car was much more affordable. It was a better deal. At least I thought it was.

Cash for a Clunker

When I told her I was going to buy my stepdad's car, my wife was very unhappy. She made it clear that it was not what she wanted. But I took control of the situation and made it clear that I knew more than she did about cars. If we got that car, it would be great—because it was cheap and had low mileage. The car was in Yuma, Arizona, and I lived in Glenwood Springs, Colorado. So I flew down there to get it.

Again my stepfather said he was not comfortable selling the car to me, but I made it clear I wanted it. I paid him cash for it, and then I took it to a car wash. They cleaned it inside and out and made it look good. I also had a mechanic check all the basics and get the car ready for the road. It took two days to get everything done, and then I drove it home.

Paint Bubbles

When I got back to Glenwood Springs, I noticed a bit of paint missing on the trunk. Then I noticed a lot of bubbles in the paint all over the roof, and the trunk, and the hood. I contacted someone at a Chevrolet dealership and asked about it. According to the guy I talked to, that particular model was known to have a paint problem. He said that almost every one of those cars had lost their paint because it all flaked off after about the fifth year. Because the car was past the warranty period, it would cost about $1,500 to have it repainted. Since the car had been in Yuma, Arizona, one of the hottest places in America, then driven to Glenwood Springs, which was very cold at the time, that probably caused the paint problem to appear more quickly.

Sliding Down the Road

The fellow at the Chevrolet dealership asked me why I bought that car. I told him my stepfather owned it and I bought it for my wife. I was shocked to learn this particular model had been a company disaster, and that Chrysler Motors had stopped manufacturing Eagle Premiers. I told him how low the mileage was and how little I spent on it, but still he didn't think I got a good deal.

The next day my wife was driving it, and she called me to say the tape player was broken and had just destroyed her music tape. More serious, she told me something was wrong with the car because it kept sliding as she drove it. That meant we needed new tires, so I got some the next day. That was another $400. I had spent $3,000 buying the car from my stepdad and another $300 in Arizona. With the new tires, I was up to $3,700. Plus the cost of a new paint job and the cost of flying to Arizona to get the car! That would have brought the cost to over $5,000.00 but I hadn't gotten it painted.

Left-Hand Signal

Within a few weeks, we drove to Southern California to see Deb's dad, who was in the hospital with a heart problem. While driving there, we experienced several problems. First, the passenger window would not roll down. Then, somewhere in Utah, the air-conditioner broke. We planned to drive through Las Vegas, and it was very hot all the way there. We drove with all the windows open, except the one on the passenger side. I pulled into a gas station to get fuel and see if I could have someone fix the problem. But it was a Sunday and no mechanics were on duty. When I opened the hood, I discovered another problem. One of the plastic tubes to the air filter was broken, so I had to put duct tape on it. I drove all over town to find an auto parts store that was open. To no avail. When we were about fifty miles from Vegas, we realized the temperature inside the car was 110 degrees. My wife was screaming and cussing at me the whole way. My son and daughter rode in the back seat, trying to keep from melting.

When we got into Vegas, the engine went kaput. I assumed it was the engine. I couldn't get the car to go more than fifteen miles per hour. And if I stopped at a stop sign or a traffic light, it kept shutting down. So I ran all the lights while going down the main street in Vegas, praying I wouldn't get pulled over.

We had to stay in Vegas for two days before anyone could fix the car. My wife and I fought the whole time. She made it clear how stupid I was and that the whole thing was entirely my fault. I couldn't disagree. I don't remember the exact cost for the repair, but it was close to $300, and according to the mechanic, it was only temporary. Now the cost for the car was approaching $4,500—and we still hadn't fixed the air-conditioning or painted the car.

When we left Vegas, the temperature was about 115 degrees. Sitting in the car was horrible. Debbie was still screaming and cussing at me. While we were on the freeway heading to California, someone drove past us and then slowed down until we got next to them. They rolled down their window, and the passenger shouted, "What kind of an idiot are you driving with your windows open!" I thought I would show them a left-hand signal, but I didn't.

A Frozen Watermelon on the Air-Conditioner

By the time we got to California, her dad was out of the hospital. While we were at her parents' home, I promised to get the air-conditioner fixed. It took another three days before anyone could perform the repair, so we had to hang out with them longer than we planned.

The company that repaired the air-conditioner made it clear that the system could not be fixed correctly because they would have to replace the entire unit—and ordering the parts would take another week, and would cost about $500. In lieu of a new air-conditioner, they set the old one to make it stay on at full blast the whole way while we drove home. The mechanic warned me that it was going to be *very* cold. That was okay with me, until we started freezing. I spent another $200 for this repair. Now I was nearing $5,000 for this lemon.

While we were in San Bernardino, temperatures were only in the low eighty range, but because we couldn't shut the air-conditioner off, we were freezing. My wife got mad at me again, and we rolled down the windows. While we were driving home and heading back toward Vegas, it got a lot hotter. We shut the windows. About an hour out of Vegas, something went very wrong. About a pound of ice fell from under the dashboard and hit my wife's foot! Then the air-conditioner shut off. When I pulled the car over and opened the hood, I saw a monster on the engine block. There was a pile of ice the size of a watermelon all over the air-conditioner. It was so large and so heavy, it actually dented the hood. I had to break the ice apart because I couldn't shut the hood without causing a bigger dent. I had to disconnect everything so the air-conditioner would stop working. It was 118 degrees when we hit Vegas, and Deb was cursing me the whole way home.

And during the trip, most of the rest of the paint came off. By the time we got home, about seventy percent of the car was missing its white finish. It looked like … well, let's just say the base primer paint was brown.

A Funny Disaster

Once we got home, I got together with my friend Doug and told him everything that happened. He thought it was one of the funniest stories he had ever heard! But he also knew I had experienced a disaster with my wife, one of the worst dustups to that point in our marriage. It did, however, offer me the opportunity for new insights in counseling to think about what I had done and what I should have done differently.

This is just one example of how my good intentions fell apart. Again I had used a good intention the wrong way. Though I was now learning how my good intentions could be headed down the wrong path, I was still blind to some things. I was still trying to control things and people, and my incentive for doing this was to benefit me rather than anyone else.

Money Down the Toilet

My experience with this car I purchased from my stepfather taught me more than just about anything else about listening to others. It reminds me to listen to others and consider their perspectives. Until then, that was something I was unwilling to do. I wanted to be in complete control. Instead of serving and honoring my wife's wishes—and trusting that even if we had spent more money buying the Camry, that extra money would have been well spent—I decided to thwart them. It was a costly mistake. Worse than the money lost was the emotional reaction I triggered in my wife!

Now there was no alternative but for Deb to go out and buy a car on her own. She went directly to the Toyota dealership and got a Camry! And the car I'd bought? I tried to give it to the dealership where she bought her Camry! They charged me fifty dollars to take it. They knew they couldn't sell it to anyone. I knew the sales person, who was a friend from church, and he said he would never try selling a car in that condition to anyone. Ever.

It cost fifty bucks to take it to a junk yard! The total cost of this great decision I made was about $5,000—and I had *not* even bought a new cassette player, replaced the air-conditioner, or had the car repainted! To fix everything that was wrong would have cost me some seven thousand big ones. But that isn't the end of my horror story. The car's transmission started causing problems the day after we got home from Southern California, and the mechanic told me I needed to replace the transmission. The transmission! That would have cost another $2,000. So to fix everything really would have cost me $9,000.

All the money I had spent had been thrown down the toilet, and now we had to buy a real car, for which I had to get a loan. Saving money on a reliable car could have been a good thing for our family, and it was certainly one of my good intentions, but when I unilaterally decided to buy my stepfather's car, my motive was all about me. I can truly admit I was a complete jerk in this whole affair.

NEW MOTIVES
ARE SO GOOD!

For the rest of my life I know I will have to pursue the goal of new motives and desires. I could continue to serve my own priorities, if they are on the right path, but if I'm not open for insights about my motive and priority, that could mess up my good intentions. Instead, I want to seek positive influences in my life and the lives of others.

So I need to be open to learn about the things that cause negative reactions. My experiences, some of them described in this book, provide positive help. I am not totally "fixed," but I am more and more open to learn about my problems and find solutions to them. Now that I am going into my sixth decade, I am in a much better situation in life regarding my personal wants and needs, and my emotional well-being. I only wish I had learned a lot of this when I was younger.

Hearing and learning from God's Spirit helps me keep gaining insights about my intentions and the motives behind them. When I honor and serve others—and trust God to give me new thoughts and desires—changes continue to come! My life attitude is now mainly positive, and if I am negative, I really want to let go of those negative thoughts quickly.

I believe I have the opportunity for life to continue to get better every year. I don't know anyone who has completely pure motives, but experiencing positive changes that influence me and others is a good way to shoot for them—and it is a great life experience.

Stay on the Middle Path

As the national sales trainer for the corporation I work for, I was sure I had the right solutions to teach people. But whenever someone went out of bounds during a training session, I was tempted to let (and sometimes did let) my motives run away from me. I would try to "fix" others, control them, judge them, or treat them like they were the problem. Sometimes I would ignore them or act like I was smarter than them. I was reverting to my old approach to good intentions.

Now, however, when someone goes off track during my training sessions, I focus more on helping them rather than reacting to them. For me, it is a matter of staying on the middle path and not going to extremes. I want to help others learn how to stand on that middle path also.

In our corporation I teach associates how to handle situations when customers go out of bounds with their reactions. I tell my associates to stand in the middle of a narrow path, and if it is a really bad event, to be willing to step into the chaos. But I tell them to be neither aggressive nor passive, the way most sales people are.

Here's what I mean: I can control my thoughts and methods. I can choose to stand in the middle of a narrow path of life events, instead of going off to the right or left. I can choose to go the middle way instead of being aggressive or passive. Leaving the middle path gets us off the track we always need to stay on.

In the past, my negative process was first to be aggressive (to fight). I would be pushy toward people, telling them what to do and how to do it. I would convey the attitude that I was annoyed, angry, or irritated. I would try to finagle people into doing what I wanted. It was an aggressive style.

When I was being passive (flight), I would go off to the left side of the narrow path. I tried to ignore things, walk away from them, and pretend I was not angry or worried. When I spoke, I didn't even look at people; I just wanted to get away from them. When I was in my passive state of mind, people were hard to tolerate. I wanted to fly away, run away, ignore, and avoid them. I was definitely not in the middle of the path.

Now during my training sessions, I show this concept on flip charts. Visual aids help us remember ideas, so at the end of this chapter I include one of the charts I use. As you look at the chart, think of the big arrow as the direction you take during a life event. When you do it on the middle narrow path, that is the small arrow headed in the same direction as the big life arrow. Going in the correct direction, and staying on the narrow path, moves you forward and upward.

The arrows in the middle of the path that point left or right lead to descriptions of how we step off the narrow path. Standing in the middle is not easy because when we stand there, we do not follow our typical personality style. We all use one of the patterns as our primary method. We start by being either aggressive or passive, fight or flight.

And when we have tried that and it doesn't work, we switch to the opposite style. Neither one works the way we hope because they are both off the narrow path. Keeping to the narrow path is very different from our natural style. But if we are going to influence people in a positive way, we need to decide to stand in the middle. Even while everything around us is going wrong, we can still choose to stand in the middle path and seek pure motives and positive changes.

Step into the Chaos

Something else is even more influential than staying on the middle path—and that is stepping into the chaos. Too often when we are standing in the middle path, if something bad happens we are not willing to step into the problem. There is a time when just standing is helpful, and there is a time when stepping into the chaos is even more helpful.

Stepping into the chaos is not being aggressive; it is being courageous. And the way to do it is not at all like our fight or flight reactions. If we don't stay on the middle path and we go right or left, we will get run over.

The drawing of a person at the bottom of the big arrow shows the direction one takes. Then two smaller boxes say, "Wrong path or thoughts" and "You get run over." If we get away from the direction we should take and disregard the middle path, we will get run over. Here is the visual illustration I use in my training:

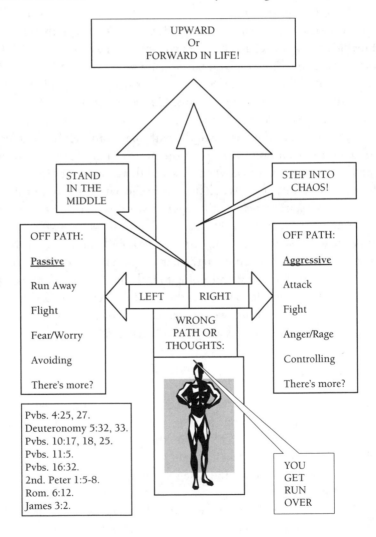

THE MIDDLE PATH BRINGS NEW LIFE PATTERNS

My old style was to think and act sometimes as if people wanted me to do unethical things. That triggered a judgmental attitude toward them. In truth, hardly any of them ever asked me to do anything unethical. That did not matter: I treated them like they had! When attendees made comments in training sessions that I disagreed with or found confusing, I would correct them. If I didn't like what they said, I assumed it was because I was smarter. I would never consider things from their point of view. I was on anything but the middle path.

Those old-style "solutions" put me in a position as the enemy. Now, however, I repeat and ask questions, and I actually listen to and consider others' perspectives. Taking the middle path (not going to extremes) and stepping into the chaos (being courageous) is a much more positive and helpful approach to influence family, friends, and customers—even enemies.

Better Motives Make Good Intentions Work

My new motive is to understand as best I can what others mean, and why. Then I can feel free to mention my own thoughts or reflect on what they say to make sure I understand them. Often that allows them to hear what they said and tweak the comment so it makes sense to everyone. This makes me a better teacher and a good influencer, not a control freak.

I also try to take better motives into my roles as a parent, husband, and friend.

I want to be open to honor others instead of trying to control them or impress them so I feel better about myself. If people want something done a certain way, but I am not in agreement, I can still serve them. And I can do it for the right reasons. Buying my wife the Toyota is a perfect example.

I may not do what someone wants if it really makes me feel uncomfortable or I am confident it is wrong. But I don't want to judge them anymore, and I don't want to control them. I would, however, like to influence them in a good way. This proves it works: "Be careful to do what is right in the eyes of everybody. If it is possible, as far as it depends on you, live at peace with everyone" (Rom. 12:17–18).

My New Motives

1. Do not judge people.
2. Try to influence everyone in a good way.
3. Prepare to do good things the way others want and need them.
4. Serve and honor others as a priority.
5. Learn to create in others a curiosity and interest to hear from me about doing things differently.

In changing my motives to make my good intentions work, I have also discovered that when I do things people want, even if I am somewhat uncomfortable about their method, it turns out to the good. I also learned that if I serve others and things don't work out, they become more open to seeing their own bad choices and realizing that in my serving them I was not the one who chose wrongly. Doing things this way now makes sense: "All a man's ways seem right to him, but the Lord weighs the heart" (Prov. 21:2).

Bad Things Turned to the Good

Bad things started to become obvious—things that were negative, scary, shocking, surprising, and totally unknown to me. But taking the middle path became an experience that was positive, intriguing, encouraging, helpful, and often surprising. So many insights started coming that I committed myself to staying on the middle path of openness. My attitude was actually changing, because I stopped trying to control what I could not control. I was not perfect at staying open—but I wanted to experience change so genuinely that I really kept at being open. When I closed myself to that, I reverted to my old style with the same bad attitudes.

Exposure!

I had been asking God to keep exposing to me things about myself that I didn't realize. For three months I experienced exactly the same event every week when I traveled. I was conducting training sessions across North America and had to travel to two or three different locations each week.

The final episode happened at the airport in Miami Beach. As I left the rental car parking lot, I asked the attendant for directions to my hotel. I wrote down and followed the directions. Within ten minutes I could tell that nothing I had been told was correct. The signs on the highways were all different, and so were the exit numbers and the road names. Nothing matched the directions. None of the street names he told me I would see on the highway appeared. Nothing was making sense, and I was getting farther and farther from my destination.

More Bad Directions

I called the hotel where I would be staying to tell them I was lost and to ask how to get there. The problem became worse, because no one at the hotel had a clue which way I needed to go to get there. They would tell me if they only knew, but no one did. Every time I got more lost, I would call the hotel and someone else would tell me a completely different way. It still didn't work!

I experienced this every week for three months while I traveled. Three months, every trip. I was always getting lost and furious! I would be driving and mentally cussing at them. I would call them back two, three, or four times to get new directions. I was so mad that even when I tried not to sound angry, I'm sure I did. Because of my tone of voice, I am sure they knew I thought they were idiots. I even had a lady stay on the phone with me for twenty minutes while she kept telling me how to get to the hotel! None of the streets were where she said they would be.

Exposed by a Mercedes Benz!

The Miami trip was the last one I handled in my "old style." Because my flight was delayed, I got to the airport at 7:00 P.M., four hours late. When I arrived, there were only a few rental cars left, but because I am a President's Circle member, I bypassed the Hertz counter and went directly to my assigned car.

I always reserve a typical midsize car, though occasionally because of my membership I get upgraded to something a bit nicer. But that night in my spot, there was a new Mercedes Benz. I thought I was in the wrong spot, so I went back to the board to make sure I had seen it correctly. I had! I then pulled out the paperwork to see if they were over-charging me. They weren't.

I had never driven a Mercedes Benz. Within five minutes, I was deflated. I couldn't figure out how to make the seat move, adjust the mirror, or turn on the air-conditioner. I couldn't figure out anything—not even how to turn on the radio. I was very mad, so I went in and complained. They said they had no other cars and I had to use that one.

I Gave Myself Bad Directions

Now we are back to where I started this story. When I left the rental car lot, I got directions to my hotel. But it was the same as always. I couldn't find the place. I called the hotel, and they gave me even worse directions. Ultimately I found the Marriott, but not the way I had been told.

When I checked in, I complained to the guy at the desk that they had given me bad directions. I said I was even told that the Marriott was on a different road.

No wonder. I was at the wrong Marriott! He gave me new directions, and I drove to the second Marriott. But when I got there, they told me I was not registered! I was nearly beside myself as I pulled out my document and showed it to the employee.

He said, "Mr. White, you might want to look at this. You registered at the Courtyard, not the Marriott."

I said, "The Courtyard *is* a Marriott."

He said Marriott did own Courtyard, but that they were not the same. He looked at the computer and gave me directions to the hotel where I was registered. It was the first hotel where I had stopped! I had to get back in my overly complicated Mercedes and drive back to that hotel. I was embarrassed—and even madder.

Still Being a Jerk!

You may think that by this time I had figured out what a jerk I was. But not yet. The next day I met with a group of sales people, and when I arrived at the office, they saw my Mercedes and assumed I was some kind of high-end, master-macho know-it-all. I had not yet met any of them, but I assumed that was what they were thinking. So we got together, and then we went out driving in their community. We used the Mercedes because none of them had cars large enough for the group.

While driving around, I let them know how much I hated this car. I explained I could not figure out how to use the air-conditioner, the radio, or the GPS system, and that I could not get the seat where I wanted it. I could not even adjust the mirrors.

After all my complaining, the guy in the front next to me said, "Here's the radio and the GPS." He touched the dashboard and a cover opened, exposing the stuff I couldn't find. I had no idea it was there all along, and all on the dashboard. Then he showed me where the rest of the things were—in the middle of the two front seats, under the arm rest, and it was full of all kinds of buttons to make everything work.

I Finally Accepted Exposure

At the end of that day I realized that in my months of experiencing the same problems (except for the Mercedes), it was because I was annoyed with events I could not control. I then realized that exposure is a good thing, and I wished I had not taken so long to find that out.

I started considering what my problems were and concluded that all the people who had given me bad directions were not hired to do what I wanted them to do. The hotels were nowhere near the airports, and I just expected everyone to know whatever I didn't know.

I also realized they had tried to meet my expectations because I made it clear that I was heading to their hotel but didn't know how to get there. They did the best they could to help me. They didn't regularly drive from the airport to their hotel, so they probably didn't know the way to the hotel any more than I did.

The rental car people didn't intentionally give me wrong information. No one can remember all the exact names and data on expressway and road signs. If you don't drive a route regularly, how can you be expected to know everything?

It became obvious that nobody was actively trying to mess up my day. I messed it up myself, because I let these events control me, instead of me controlling my thoughts.

Proof of My Problem

Still, my getting lost did not end there. On my next two trips I again got lost, but I took control of my thoughts and found myself delighted that I had stepped out of my old pattern. I actually enjoyed getting bad directions because it proved to me that I had control over my thoughts and my anger. I spent the time driving around, enjoying the views and feeling certain that no one was trying to be a problem for a jerk like me.

I thanked God for exposing me, instead of letting me remain stuck on my bad path. Because it works out to the good, I still want to experience exposure of the bad things I am unaware of.

Since those eventful trips, I have not had another one that has taken me off the middle path of openness and exposure. I have taken many trips since, and I believe I can say I am on a new and better pathway!

Perspectives and Opinions That Are Right and Wrong

Many bad things turned to the good, but there were still some things that kept me stuck. I did not understand what was wrong and how I was processing things. I needed much patience and determination to stay committed to discovering additional problems with my perspectives, opinions, and behaviors.

I thought some of my perspectives were positive, but I was unaware I had negative thoughts, feelings, and reactions about those perspectives. That is why I was stuck in a rut.

Some Perspectives Were a Mess

This is more proof of how solutions can still blind one to good intentions. My perspectives, which I saw as solutions, fell into two groups. The first were from a negative perspective, and the second, from a positive perspective. Interestingly, both were wrong, and both caused negative reactions within me. But getting insight about them caused yet more positive changes in me.

I was committed to gaining insights from reading the Bible, listening to some friends, reading books, and journaling my thoughts. All those helped provide positive insights about why my perspectives needed changing. Being patient—and having faith that God would give me true insights—did provide new and helpful ways to look at things.

My Negative Perspectives

Perspective: Because it took time to find insights and solutions, I did not think I had enough time or patience to wait. That caused reactions.

Perspective: I assumed things would fail because of the time it took for a solution.

Reaction: My perspectives about time issues caused a flight/fight, passive/aggressive syndrome. I would go into the fight/aggressive posture with pushing, pulling, pressuring, controlling, manipulating, and whatever else it took to make things work quickly.

Reaction: Or I would go into the flight/passive position and be fearful and worried, causing me to run away, hide, withdraw, retreat, ignore, and minimize my problems.

Perspective: Hearing from others about my faults was not helpful or accurate, because they did not understand why I did or did not do things.

Reaction: I did not even consider insights from those I judged as idiots or anyone else that irritated me.

Reaction: I rejected their comments instead of looking for a nugget of truth.

Reaction: It was hard to find a nugget of truth in someone's foul comments toward me, so why bother wasting time thinking about it?

Perspective: Sometimes I had no idea how to change, or I did not even think I could change.

Reaction: So I ignored my problem and thought it was not a big deal.

Reaction: Some of my problems led to shame and guilt, which I ignored or hid.

Reaction: There were times it seemed pointless to even consider change. Change seemed so futile.

Reaction: There is no point listening to people's comments about my faults, since change is fruitless.

My Positive Perspectives

Perspective: I was committed to doing things that proved I was on the right track.
Reaction: But when those things did not work, I blamed others.
Perspective: My intentions were good and appropriate, and my expectations were valid.
Reaction: I got angry with others when they did not meet my expectations.
Reaction: I kept raising the bar and putting more pressure on myself and everyone else. Then guilt took over.
Perspective: I felt that if I always told people what they needed to hear, they would do the right things.
Reaction: Yet when they did not do the right things, I judged them as irresponsible or stupid.
Perspective: Fixing problems was my purpose and responsibility in life.
Reaction: When I could not fix the problem and could not figure out why, I did not consider the perspectives of others.
Reaction: I was sure my perspectives were accurate and that others with different perspectives were wrong.
Reaction: Either I pushed and pressured myself and others, or I would give up and not bother.
Perspective: My goals and intentions created plans that I thought fit biblical concepts, so I knew I was doing the right things.
Reaction: When things went wrong, I got angry and judged people, because I thought they were not as godly as me.
Reaction: I quit hanging around those kinds of people.
Reaction: I would use biblical verses to justify myself and accuse others.

Because I thought my insights were correct, I completely missed the concept of *unconditional love.* My perspectives and goals were meant for me only, and I used others to fill my needs and desires, thinking I was on the right track.

Good Turned Bad

I vowed to be a dad who was actively present in his children's lives. I also wanted to find a mentor to teach me how to make life work better and learn how to be a great husband and father, because my dad wasn't around to teach me those things.

Later, I was committed to get married and stay married. I was not going to put my family through a divorce like my parents had done to me. I learned to cook, keep house, wash and iron my clothes, wash the dishes, and clean the toilets and windows so my future wife would not feel like I used her as a slave. I would do whatever it took ethically to be a good provider, so my wife could stay home and be a great mom. At twenty-one I was still committed to staying a virgin for the benefit of my future wife.

I discussed my intentions about being a great husband with my close friend Bob Donnelly. I remember telling Bob that my future wife would be the most important person to me—more important than anyone else on the planet. I remember people saying I would be a great husband because of my attitude and intentions. I even volunteered regularly to babysit for my friends Bill and Jenny Telliard so I could practice being good with kids. Their kids called me Uncle Steve because I spent so much time watching and caring for them.

I had other good intentions. I wasn't going to be just another macho man. I wanted to be well balanced: strong yet tender, manly yet humble. At twenty-one I had developed some good spiritual disciplines, and I was committed to continuing them. But I was not going to be a religious weirdo with my Christianity.

I had amassed a lot of good intentions that were very clear and very dear to me. I found a mentor, Mike Gemme. Mike was going to be the guy who showed me how to be a good man and a great husband and dad. I failed to mention that to Mike, but still I had expectations for both him and myself.

There was nothing wrong with many of my intentions; actually they were good. The problem was not my good intentions. The problem was that I needed all these desires to fall in line in order to feel good about myself and to fill the needs of my heart. I thought I had been screwed over by some people, and I didn't want to be like them. I wanted to be different.

Wanting to be different is fine, but what I did not realize was that I was no different from anyone else, even those I thought had screwed me over. Perhaps many of these people had meant well, but if they did, I surely missed it.

The Odds Are Slight

What are the odds that my mother and father did not want to be good parents? What are the odds that my relatives were not trying to be helpful? What are the odds that those in the Navy were not trying to be heroes? What are the odds that everyone on this planet does not want to be a hero, do the right things, and have good intentions?

The chances for all of these things are very slight. Yet I was directing my own story in my own movie—and using others as my actors to make life work the way I wanted. I was trying to get everyone to meet my needs, and in doing so I created a conflict of interest with others. I was always serving myself or using them to serve me.

I was not aware that all of this was going on within me. I was blind about my motives—again, because my intentions were so good. I was blinded by my good intentions. My pride and arrogance were the foundational problems. I thought I could be a grander version of my father, better and smarter in everything. But my arrogance prevented me from experiencing the very things I wanted to achieve, and I thought that those who noticed and told me about my arrogance were just plain stupid.

I did not see the consequences of my prideful outlook. But that has changed. Now I see my problems and I do not want to walk that earlier path. Rather, I want to help others avoid the snares I experienced and help set them free of the same defeating patterns.

HUMPTY DUMPTY SAT ON A WALL

My intentions were good, but they were not born of real wisdom. I can see that now. Looking back at my experiences through the lens of time and the pain of the past clarifies this. Instead of wisdom, my intentions came from resentment about negative events I blamed on my parents, others, or life in general. My parents may have been partially culpable, but it had not occurred to me that maybe they were not the issue. Maybe others were not responsible for my pain. Maybe life in general was not the culprit.

Because I was determined to shield those I loved from events like those I had experienced, my intentions seemed good. Yet my arrogance kept my good intentions at bay. I did not recognize I was on a slowly sinking boat. I loved my wife and kids, but it wasn't the kind of love that God has for us, which is unconditional.

From an early age I missed all the clues about what it takes to make things work out. I lacked the necessary social tools, and I did not have enough wisdom to support my specific intentions. But I did have passion! I had climbed a great wall to the top, thinking I was where I needed to be. But I was like Humpty Dumpty on the verge of a fall. I thought I was serving others, but in truth I was serving myself and using others to meet my needs.

My intentions seemed so good, so clear, and so noble, that for twenty-five years I unknowingly continued to manipulate everyone and everything around me. My goals and expectations were no secret; I told many people about what I expected for my life and my family. Many encouraged me and said I was on the right track. It had not occurred to me that arrogance, pride, and cluelessness were driving my life—or that response to my pain fueled all my intentions.

Missing the mark failed to lower my expectation to achieve my intentions. In fact, it propelled me toward them even faster and more blindly. My anger began to accelerate, and my life became intense. Others may have realized I was about to fall off the wall, but it escaped me until …

Humpty Dumpty Had a Great Fall

Justifying my selfishness and minimizing my problems became less of a pattern for me. Experiencing real forgiveness from God and his love helped me see that I should serve the interest of others and not my own. When people told me what I was doing wrong, I listened to see where I went off track and why things were not working out the way I wanted. I started looking for the nugget of truth in everything others said to me and about me. I also asked God for insight. This new approach was not easy, but I directed my attention to solving my own problems and not to solving others'. This started bringing about insights. That was a great fall in a very good way.

I also realized that the arrogant attitude I expressed when I was off track usually convinced others there was no point in telling me what was wrong with me. Why invest the effort? I would not listen. But now things were starting to change. I thought, What if I had looked honestly at the outcomes of my life and then asked, Why is this failing? What if I waited for God's insights instead of coming up with my own notions of what was right and wrong? What if I was honest with myself about my failings instead of blaming others? Could I reverse the process of always defending myself and judging others? Would

I stay committed to controlling my thoughts? What is the problem: my good intentions, or the way I go about them?

Humpty's Dirt Clods

One day, while we were on a run, my friend Doug revealed something about my good intentions. I said, "I just need to keep telling my family about their shortcomings and they will finally get it and get in line with my intentions. I need to repeat myself a thousand and one times until they get it!"

Mockingly, he said, "Why don't you just do the same thing one thousand and two times? I am sure they will get it then." He looked at me like I was stupid—and would always be stupid!

It sunk in. "I am stupid," I said. "What have I been thinking? I thought I was throwing out a jewel of a thought."

He said, "No, it was a dirt clod." (Actually he called it something else.)

Humpty's Blind to Facts

There were patterns of thoughts I found myself pursuing, and it was tempting to justify myself because my intentions seemed to make sense. The following insights were helpful because I was finally open to considering new patterns of thought.

Wanting to be a great husband and father was a good thing, but I had been blind to the fact that I was doing it wrong. How would I know how to make things work in my family when I never learned this from my parents? I did not have the right tools to be a great parent and husband. I needed to learn from someone, but I had no models.

I tried to control people and make them cooperate. I did not consider that everyone else had their own agendas, and most were in conflict with mine.

I did not know my motives were rooted in bitterness, anger, and envy. I needed to allow others to reveal my motives and be open to hearing and considering what they said, without excusing or justifying myself.

For forty-five years, trying to prevent painful experiences had not worked. But connecting to God and experiencing freedom from my old patterns provided joy and peace, even during hard times. Joy and peace became my priorities.

Humpty Dumpty Became Wiser

Other helpful insights were these:

- Getting to the root of a problem became important to me. No longer would I focus on surface issues and symptoms.
- I knew I could not always do it alone.
- I spent more time considering what my problems and faults were instead of focusing on anyone else's problems.
- I needed to let God change me from the inside, instead of trying to control outward symptoms.
- I had neither the desire, willpower, nor energy to continue trying to manage my negative behaviors with a new set of rules and expectations. I needed a core change from within.

After those insights and a new set of intentions, my focus on everyone else became less important. Now I was looking at myself. A shift was occurring in my heart and mind, and I knew it was real. I really wanted to stop falling off the wall.

FIXING SPOUSES MAKES YOU THEIR ENEMY

This story is about a husband and wife who were my next-door neighbors. I have their permission to tell this story, and I want to tell it because it shows how I used to handle things with my wife. I thought I knew the solution to any specific problem she had. I thought that all I had to do was keep on track with my good intentions to eliminate her difficulties and be her solution. I found out later that this approach made me her enemy.

One day I was sitting on my deck when I saw my neighbor on his deck with a drink in his hand. We were about ten yards apart. I asked him about his day, and he told me he had to take his wife to the emergency room, but they found nothing wrong with her. I knew from an earlier conversation with the two of them that money was a big issue at the time, and that she was having trouble finding a job. I invited him over for a drink and conversation. Until then, we had only talked from our decks.

First Attract, Then Attack

He came over to my town home and began describing his wife's ailment. He discussed his concerns about her physical and emotional states. He said his wife went about dealing with money problems all wrong. He described how he dealt with questions of money, and in his mind he was very good at that. Naturally, he and his wife were complete opposites in how they dealt with solving financial problems. I told him I thought this is all part of God's sense of humor (I don't really believe this) for opposite personalities to be attracted to each other. It's first attract, then attack! From there it does not take long before husbands and wives start hating their differences.

A Complete Whiff

My neighbor told me how he repeatedly kept trying to teach his wife how to think differently on all sorts of topics. This was his commitment. In five minutes he said the same thing at least four times: "I have to make her see it. Whatever it takes, I have got to make her understand what to do."

Obviously he was driven by good intentions. He wanted the best for his wife, and he knew how to get it. If she would only listen to him, she might get it! He believed that if he kept at it, in time she would come around.

This all sounded a lot like me and the way I tried to make my wife understand what to do.

I tried explaining to him that I had adopted the same approach—and what I had learned through my failures. I told him I would do things differently now. I talked to him about how I learned to listen without trying to fix everything. "It's best to just listen, reflect, and love them," I said.

I also mentioned that when my wife felt I had heard and understood her, she often figured out her own solutions. I didn't need to say anything! Sometimes I might be able to display the kind of thought-processing that could help her, but I tried waiting until she asked for help. My goal was to listen, reflect, love, and support her—not to fix her.

My neighbor nodded as if he understood me. Then he said, "Yep, I've got to do whatever it takes to get her to think differently. I have to keep at this and keep telling her what her problem is and convince her!" It was a complete whiff; everything I said went right over his head. But he had the best of intentions. This was her fourth marriage, and I am sure this man was not going to be the one to fix her! Although he did not see it that way, in her view he had become the enemy.

I had been on the same track as my neighbor. But after hearing his story I was not angry with him, nor did I judge him for being just like I once was. Instead of trying to fix him and expect him to change, I was more focused on revealing my problems and what grief they caused with my wife. I walked alongside my neighbor and his problem over time, and it kept him open and honest with me about how he was interacting with his wife. He knew I had been in the same boat.

SECTION 4

CAN YOU SPARE SOME CHANGE?

The stories in this section are about what led me to control my thoughts and stay on the middle path instead of being aggressive or passive, using fight or flight symptoms as a reaction to events and people. I also had new motives about serving, honoring, and prioritizing others' needs instead of my own and being open to hear from people and to tell friends about my struggles. Remembering these concepts can help us if we control ourselves.

A PIECE OF REBAR LEARNED HOW TO FLY

Four of us were sitting out on my back deck preparing to barbeque our dinner. My friends Jim Dryden, Brad Janssen, Sonny Canterbury, and I had filled our glasses and poured a bottle of red wine in a nice decanter that was a Christmas gift from my son. The decanter sat in the middle of the table surrounded by filled wine glasses.

While we sat and talked, Sonny noticed a large plastic bag about thirty feet up in an Aspen tree off the deck. He could tell it had been there a long time because it was dirty and ripped and stuck all around a few branches. He asked me why I hadn't removed it. I said there was no way I was climbing the tree to get rid of it. We continued to talk and enjoy the wine and appetizers.

At some point Sonny got up and walked through the house and didn't come back out on the deck. A few minutes later I saw him out by the tree. He had gone to his truck and retrieved a four-foot piece of rebar.

I asked him what he was doing, and he said he was going to get the bag down.

I had no idea how he planned to do this, so I sat with the two others and we continued talking. Then we heard a noise in the tree. Sonny had thrown the rebar at the bag, but it just hit the branches. I couldn't figure how he thought throwing a steel rod at a bag in a tree would work, but I ignored him and continued talking with my friends.

Glass Exploded!

A minute later a crash on my table caused a glass explosion. The rebar had flown out of the tree about ten feet above the deck, landed on the table, broken my wine decanter, and shattered some glass that pierced my leg. (I was wearing a pair of shorts.) Wine was all over the table and the deck, all over me and my guests, and my leg was bleeding.

Standing below the deck, Sonny couldn't see what had happened, but he sure heard the commotion. He came up, said he was sorry, and handed me a $100 bill.

I gave it back to him, and he made it clear he was going to buy me a new decanter.

I told him that was not going to happen.

Jim has an aggressive personality, and he got ticked at Sonny. He yelled at him and started telling him what to do.

Brad, on the other hand, has a passive personality. He said he was going to buy me new glasses and a decanter, and he began cleaning up the mess. Then he said he would provide everything soon and that he was so sorry that this happened. Brad was teary eyed, and so uncomfortable with the situation, he didn't even talk to Sonny. He just kept telling me he was going to take care of the mess.

Meanwhile Jim kept deriding Sonny and telling him he better not let this happen again.

A Middle Path in a Bad Event

After about three minutes I told everyone to just sit down and stop talking about the problem. It was my turn to deal with this issue. I told Sonny I really loved him as a friend, and that I was not even mad at him, because it was obvious that he did not want this to happen. He did destroy a gift from my son, and my leg was bleeding, but none of that was what Sonny planned.

I was actually pleased with myself for not being mad at him. It was not the way I would have acted in the past. I told Sonny he did not have to replace anything and that I appreciated him helping to clean things up.

What Sonny did caused more of a problem with Jim and Brad than with me. I was amazed at what I had learned from God about how he loves us regardless of what we do wrong. Because I experienced and believed that, I found myself able to love others like God loves me. I felt God would use this situation to teach Jim, Brad and Sonny what I had learned.

As for Brad, every time someone did something wrong, he was always trying to make things right. He wanted to take control to make sure everyone felt good. By promising to pay me, he was trying to fix what Sonny did wrong.

But I took another point of view. I thought God wanted to use the situation to teach the four of us something important: We all need to experience a change in attitude and how we handle bad events. When things go wrong, we all need to find our way to the middle path.

Sonny needed to figure out why he did things like this. This was not the first time Sonny's control issues had caused problems. He wanted to fix everyone and everything. He needed to learn that you can't fix everything; you need to stand in the middle of bad events.

Lesson Learned

Because of a plastic bag hung up in a tree, the four of us got to walk through a scenario I had been thinking and talking about for months. It was an object lesson about the kind of changes we all need.

Earlier I would have used a situation like this to prove what a jerk somebody was, and I would have made sure they felt lousy about what they had done. I would have used sarcasm and ridicule to prove I was smarter than whoever did something stupid.

That was the way I would have acted in the past, but in this case I just started laughing. It struck me as funny how God uses problems to expose our true natures. After that, we were all laughing.

The next Christmas Sonny bought me a very expensive new wine decanter, which I still use. It reminds me of lessons learned, including my need to control my thoughts, to help others instead of being interested only in solving my problems, to be open with a group of friends, and to stand in the middle path instead of being aggressive or passive.

CHANGE ON THE RIGHT PATH

Remembering the good and insightful lessons in my past experiences (like the episode with Sonny and the rebar) keeps me on the right path. I write everything in my journal so I can remember what happened. Here are some of the thoughts I have recorded in it:

Remembering what I have done in certain situations gives me a good awareness of what I do wrong and what I can do to prevent a similar problem.

Change for its own sake is not the goal. A change in thinking and behavior can bring a solution, or it can go down the wrong path. Before, I would have relied on my own opinions and assumptions, but now when I stay open for insights I am able to learn more about the right path. Staying open to insights makes me aware of the dilemmas I am responsible for.

I create some dilemmas because of my own personality issues, which allow me to feel comfortable or confident even when I am off track. An example would be my desire to control things or people. Because this is my natural tendency, I push harder and think it is a good thing. But I have learned that it is not! Yes, I still want to influence people, but only in a good and non-manipulative way.

Sometimes events work out and sometimes they do not. Either way, I used to do whatever it took to make my life enjoyable. Now I want peace, joy, and freedom.

What personality strengths I have are real and good, but when those strengths are exaggerated they turn into failures. I now try to stay open to hearing about my problems and failures, as well as other people's reactions to the things I do.

Failures tend to make me go passive or aggressive. What I need to do, however, is to keep standing in the middle of the narrow life path. That is the only thing that really helps.

I have faith in God and his unconditional love. And I realize we must remember God's love if we want to influence others positively.

I have to stop assuming that others are always causing my problems. I certainly cause my own share of them. Other people could be in the same boat. I must let go of blaming and judging them.

No one can control world events, or even all of our own life's events. But we can control our thoughts!

Setting my mind and heart on heavenly things—instead of earthly things—is the best way to control my thoughts. Philippians 4:8 instructs us to dwell on admirable things: "Finally, brothers, whatever is true, whatever is noble, whatever is right, whatever is pure, whatever is lovely, whatever is admirable—if anything is excellent or praiseworthy—think about such things."

The rules I used to live by were the root of my later problems. They provided bad motives because they were thoughtless reactions. I need to remember not to do that ever again!

I am human. Even when things aren't working for me because of others, I can still take responsibility for my thoughts, feelings, and reactions. Let others be responsible for their own problems; I am responsible for mine.

Remembering the lessons I have learned is critical to maintaining the path I want to stay on.

Justifications That Kept Me on the Wrong Path

These are thoughts I struggled with when I wanted to change:

- It is not fair that I should be the one to change first.
- Why can't others admit their problems, too? Why should I be the one who needs to change?
- Others are not doing their part, so why should I have to focus on mine?
- This is a mutual relationship, and that means we both need to work on it at the same time. It is not fair!

One last thing about sparing change for solutions: I spent a lot of time and energy trying to change outward behaviors. I thought acting differently might change me quickly, and that would be the beginning of something permanent.

There were times I thought this worked, but my behavior did not stay changed for long. I eventually realized to make a lasting transformation, I needed to change from the inside out. Controlling outward behavior was a nice thought, but it was not a wise one. I now see that real change in character has to start in the heart.

WHAT HAPPENS IN VEGAS STAYS IN VEGAS—OR NOT

I was scheduled to speak at our company's national convention in Las Vegas in November, 2005. My first session was a large one on Monday. My second session was on Wednesday.

The month before the convention I experienced an ongoing struggle with my boss about how I should handle those sessions. We disagreed over this, but then we disagreed over many things almost daily. This battle was part of a normal pattern that had taken place for years prior to every convention or major conference.

I find it interesting that I have had a different boss before every major convention. The man I worked for at this time was in upper management, the director of my division. He spent a half hour on the phone ridiculing me, yelling and cussing at me, telling me I was screwing up everything. What was he referring to? The shade of color for the wording of a title on one PowerPoint slide. One slide! He was also furious because the bullet points on that slide were one-fourth of an inch off-line from where he thought they should be.

At the start, the company's Las Vegas convention was the worst ever for me. I had to spend a lot of time talking to my friend, Doug, about issues surrounding the convention. During the previous month we had talked at length at least four times about the problems I was having with my boss. A week before the convention Doug said, "This is way over the top. Sit back and watch God work!"

As I thought about all the previous conventions and conferences, I knew this one could turn out positively, as the others had done. But I feared doing some things wrong and ruining the meetings. I found myself replaying negative thoughts of being a failure in everyone's eyes. I also imagined that God would intervene—by exposing all of my faults and embarrassing me in front of the whole assembly.

Fortunately, I let those thoughts go when I remembered all the other times when the outcomes had been positive. I was excited in a good way, but still a bit nervous about my presentations.

The Rio Was Not Grand

We stayed at the Las Vegas Rio Hotel and Casino. Mid-morning on Monday, it was close to the time for my session when things went very wrong. I walked into the conference room to check on the microphone headset and the projector, and to make sure my computer worked with their wiring. But the people at the Rio had not set up my stage, and there was none of the equipment my boss was supposed to request—and no employees in the room. I found out they had been setting up all the small rooms for the afternoon sessions. My session was the big one, and they had done nothing to prepare for it.

I left the room and found my boss—the person who had been assaulting me on the phone—and I told him what was going on. He accused me of being the problem because I should have started setting everything up myself instead of coming to him, complaining and wasting his time!

I was furious. After all, I did not have the equipment; it belonged to the hotel. Further, I had no permission to use it.

There was less than a half hour to get set up, and I couldn't even find any hotel employees to bring the equipment to the room. In his most understanding way, my boss told me it was my problem and that I had to deal with it. The main thing was not to bother him about it.

I stormed away to find someone in the hotel. It took them twenty minutes to start setting up the equipment, and my session was supposed to start in ten minutes. It didn't. It started twenty-five minutes late. Everyone in the room waited patiently, though I knew many of them were annoyed.

Because we had so many training sessions going on each day, the timing for each presentation was critical. None of the presenters could go past their allotted time, or the entire convention schedule would get off kilter.

I was the national sales trainer, and my session was the second largest one of the week. My whole session was structured around a fifteen-minute movie clip about a salesman for the Watkins Company named Bill Porter. The movie starred William Macy as Bill Porter. Porter was born with cerebral palsy, but instead of going on disability, he became a door-to-door salesman for his company. His determination led him to become its top seller. All the key points I had planned in the training session were in the video and set the stage for the session. I was sure I was about to step into not only a disaster but also a humiliating experience. It got even worse.

It became obvious that my boss, who was the director of training, had forgotten to tell the hotel to prepare my session. This guy was a piece of work. He even went to the corporation's senior vice president and tried to make it look like I was the one who screwed up. When I finally walked to the front of the room to begin the session, the VP said something very rude to me. I was so mad, I started shaking. I considered grabbing the microphone and telling the group who caused this disaster and what the VP had just said to me. I even thought of telling the group while on stage that I was quitting my job.

And I Was Not Grand at the Rio

I wrestled with the temptation to quit my job right there, but I let that thought go. I started the session and spoke to the audience, trying to explain as calmly as I could that there was a problem with setting up the equipment and that I had no control over it. I turned on my video system—and it didn't work. The hotel employees had to spend another five minutes trying to get it to work, but it never did. Then as I started to speak, the sound system went haywire.

Forty minutes of the seminar were wasted. The attendees would miss all the key points. I didn't even have time to tell them why the video was supposed to be shown, so I told them to go out and buy the DVD. I couldn't even give them the handouts I had planned to distribute because the director had also decided—without telling me—that they would not be allowed because they would exceed the company's budget. I didn't know he had not printed my documents before the session started. I suspect he had forgotten to print my handouts, and saying he had decided not to print them was his way to avoid embarrassment. So I had to abandon the second half of the presentation.

I was supposed to have ninety minutes for my presentation, but I got to talk for only fifty. Without the film clip, nothing made any sense. In my mind the session was a total failure, a complete disaster. Usually after speaking in a session such as this, I would mingle with the attendees and answer any questions. Not this time. When it ended, I went upstairs and planned to bail out of the entire conference for the day, including dinner. I was so humiliated, I decided I would not show up in public. I was seriously considering telling my boss to take the job and shove it, and then fly back to Colorado.

In my hotel room I spent a few hours walking through all that had happened. Previous conferences had had good outcomes. What had gone wrong? A feeling of terror came over me about the other session coming up on Wednesday. As I thought about that, and all the technical support I needed for it, I decided I would not use videos or any other electronic equipment. I would lower the standard of my session so I could not possibly be screwed over again. I decided to make the next session almost a non-event, just so I could protect myself from failure.

As I considered it all, I decided to exercise some courage and go back downstairs and rejoin everyone during the cocktail hour to try to overcome my humiliation. But once I got downstairs, I was very uncomfortable talking to people and decided to eat dinner on my own.

Sweating in the Cold

The next morning I went outside and sat by the pool. The conference was beginning for the day, but it could go on without me. It was not pool weather; it was so cold, no one else was out there. Even so, I noticed I was sweating.

While I sat out at the pool, I decided to call my friend Doug. Meanwhile, another friend, Steve Edney, came out and sat with me. He had seen what happened the day before. I phoned Doug and told him about the whole thing.

He listened and reflected with me. Recognizing that what had happened was a genuine disaster, Doug asked me what I was going to do for the rest of the convention.

I mentioned quitting my job. I told him I was supposed to do another huge session on Wednesday called "The Complete Salesperson: Going from Good to Great." It was a really good session, but I was losing interest in doing it.

Then Doug asked me an odd question: "What do you think God had to do with all this stuff?"

I don't remember how I answered.

Doug kept asking me really good questions about where God was in all of this. Does he care about our lives and fears? Is he always available to redeem things and do the miraculous?

I reassessed things. I stopped repeating the disaster in my mind. I remembered the times God had rescued me. And I realized that every previous national convention I had ever done had been marked by similar scenarios where things did not work out. Yet God had worked in the situation and made me effective for the attendees.

Doug suggested that I spend some time with God and ask for insights about this whole issue. He told me this fiasco might just be an incredible setup for me to knock it out of the park on Wednesday.

I could handle this in different ways. I could go off in a rage. I could bail out and choose a place to hide. Or I could stand in the battle zone and not lower the standard for the next session.

Doug said he could see me walking attendees through what I experienced on Monday, and emphasizing the process of passive or aggressive choices about behaviors. He hit the nail on the head of every thought I had wrestled with the day before.

It became clear that I should tell the group about my experience Monday—not what my bosses had said or done, but how things went wrong. I could tell them about how I felt, why I hid from everyone last night, and what my thoughts were about getting angry or giving up.

Revealing the real story about what they had all seen would help me emphasize the point of going from good to great. I was pleased with the presentation I was seeing in my mind, and I was sure God would make the presentation realistic and powerful. It wouldn't matter if all the technical stuff failed again, because this would be further proof of what it takes for the average salesperson and go from good to great. It is our character and our true desire to help others that keeps a good salesperson pressing on in difficult situations.

The Dog Wagged the Tail This Time

When I did the session on Wednesday, I started with the story about Monday's complete failure. I kept my presentation positive, and colleagues were applauding the concepts I discussed. I had never experienced people applauding during a training session about sales concepts, but in this one it happened. It was mind-blowing. When I finished the workshop, the room erupted with applause, and many people came up to me afterward telling me it was incredible. Even my director told me it was great!

The opening slide of my PowerPoint presentation was providential, for the phrase I had written on the first slide was, "Without a vision of who you can be, you will settle for what you can do, and that is easier—but then the tail is wagging the dog."

Later that day the director and the VP did a session together and spent a lot of time talking about my seminar and convincing people to get involved with me. As I sat in the back of the room, I found it hard to believe what they were saying. I was in awe about how God works. Walking with God is an adventure, but it is not always an easy walk on a grassy meadow.

Years later I did another conference called the "Growth Summit" in Chicago. This conference had about twenty speakers, all of them addressing one topic. Some of the people from the Las Vegas convention were also there. During breaks, five people came up and told me they realized that most of the topics at the Chicago conference were things I had created and had been teaching for a decade. For me, this signaled a real cultural change in our company.

Over the years I have participated in many conventions. Whenever I teach or speak at these meetings, I want to help people improve not only their jobs, but also their lives. Few of the conventions went perfectly; at almost every one the bosses created difficulties for me. But the conventions all had positive outcomes, and at each one I was honored for the perspective I brought on being open and willing to walk the middle path through bad events. It really has been true in my life that walking with God is an adventure.

Here are the concepts I have learned because of my experiences at conventions:

- Be open for insights and exposure.
- Get to the roots of my wounds.
- Connect the dots between my attitudes and behaviors.
- Make a priority of the relationship between me, God, and others.
- Remember and replay the positive thoughts, not the negatives.
- Tell close friends about my struggles.
- Focus on the one thing I have control over: my thoughts!

I WANTED BOSSES TO SPARE SOME CHANGE, BUT I HAD TO INSTEAD

I Was Not Taking Over

I have experienced some negative relations with every boss I've ever had. No one is perfect, me included. The really bad stuff had to do with my anger or emotional pain caused by my bosses' criticism, controlling attitudes, and verbal assaults. They were not doing anything illegal in the workplace or immoral with their authority, but at times the way they treated me was scandalous.

Almost everyone has encountered bad situations at work. Many of those were caused not by the job itself, but by the boss. How many of us have gotten angry or annoyed at their boss? How many have thought of quitting? Or of taking the boss outside and beating some sense into him? Most bosses experience the same things with employees. I have been down both paths numerous times.

Many bosses have expectations and demands about what it takes for employees to be on the right track. When things don't work the way a boss wants, it can become a major problem between him and employees. We as bosses may have good intentions about managing people, but we may be blind to how we have a negative influence on them and prevent things from working out to the good. This applies not just to the workplace, but also to life at home, church, or life in general. That is how I was with my wife.

Over my years as the national sales trainer for our company, I had good relationships with the employees—and eventually I did have a positive relationship with every boss. But most bosses felt they had to make sure I knew who was in charge. Some may have thought I put their jobs at risk because I had been asked by upper management to serve as the director of training, a position I turned down three times. I wanted to stay where I was. To me that seemed the best way I could contribute to the company and the sales force. Attendees at my training sessions made so many positive comments about me to my bosses, they may have felt I was more popular than they and that I was taking over. They would make sarcastic remarks that they did not believe what others were saying about me.

I heard from people I trained that when they told my bosses how much they liked my training materials, some bosses would ridicule, criticize, or try to make me look stupid on stage in front of groups. My bosses had no idea that when they said such things, people would come up to me after a session and tell me the boss was the problem, and that I ought to take their job. But, as you are about to see, there was a good outcome within me.

What Do I Have Control Over?

At times I went down the wrong path by getting mad at my bosses and attacking them in my mind. Sometimes I felt like running away and hiding in a cave. Many times I really wanted to resign. It was always a choice between fight or flight. And I was not always the innocent party. At times I talked behind their backs. I might not have ridiculed them or tried to undermine them openly, but I did not protect them from the negative comments of others. Nor did I tell others about my bosses' good points and strengths. Sometimes I played the victim card and made my bosses the problem. I so hated the way these guys treated me, I was dominated by negative thoughts.

Because I stayed stuck on negative thoughts, I came to a place of such frustration and disappointment about my job that it became the major issue in my life. As I would process things and discuss them with my friends, my job situation became more and more of a problem. I could not change my bosses; the only part of life I had any control over was my thoughts. But these were not under control. Instead, I would indulge in negative thoughts and judge others. I thought that would free me from my ongoing irritation because I knew *they* were the problem. It was fight or flight. When anything negative happened, that would trigger all my previous bad experiences and I would replay them over and over.

I was hooked line and sinker by a stinker! And I was the stinker, not my bosses! Eventually I came to a place of wanting to let go of all the negative thoughts and feelings. This came about when I realized what I actually had control over: my thoughts!

Controlling our thoughts provides freedom from being stuck on negative thoughts—and letting them control our lives. There is another visual tool you will see below that I have used in my training for a long time. I call it the Event Wheel.

The Event Wheel

The Event Wheel you will see in this chapter shows how we process experiences in our mind. The event is the first trigger. Events trigger thoughts, thoughts cause feelings, and feelings bring about actions and reactions.

Let's assume that reactions are the negative outcome and that actions are the positive. Negative events cause negative thoughts, negative thoughts cause negative feelings, and negative feelings trigger negative reactions. Positives do the opposite.

Think of some really bad event that happened in your past. Then think of how many times you have replayed that event in your mind. Hundreds? Thousands? Millions? How long have you replayed it? Days or weeks? Months or years? That is what we do—and that is what we need to control.

There is no way we can control world events, or even many events of our personal life. We have complete control only of our thoughts.

Even then it is certainly not easy to control our thoughts. We each experience tragic and heartbreaking events, and it is hard not to think about them in negative ways. If we stay focused on remembering and replaying the tragedy over a long period of time, that will have a deep, negative impact on our feelings. And those negative feelings will cause negative reactions.

Staying on the Event Wheel and constantly recycling that event and those negative thoughts can turn our hearts and minds into disasters. The technical result of repeatedly replaying thoughts is a problem called a synaptic gap. Rethinking events carves a rut or a trough into our mind. Some events cause so much negative thinking, the synaptic gap prevents some people from being mentally healthy.

In my experiences it has taken huge amounts of time, energy, effort, and commitment to control negative thoughts. But had I not battled against them, they would have wiped me out. Although it exhausted me, it brought me to the path that provides freedom from despair, anger, and judgment.

Replaying Positive Thoughts

My divorce provides a good example of this. It was heartbreaking. I lost my daughter and son. For days I was in a deplorable condition. But I eventually chose not to focus on all the negatives regarding my wife and marriage. I wanted to understand my problems and learn to change, so instead of replaying what was wrong with the marriage, I replayed the things I learned after I discovered what was wrong with me. These were positive thoughts about how my changes could have a helpful influence on myself and others.

Discovering my problems was encouraging. We all have problems. But I discovered that if I could experience change, others could too. My experience could potentially help others also become positive. Those are the thoughts I replayed rather than the negative thoughts about the divorce.

I knew that God loved me, even though I was full of problems. It took time, but I started loving myself again by replaying thoughts about people I loved. Those are thoughts I plan to replay for the rest of my life.

A Promise from God

In the apostle Paul's letter to the Romans, starting in chapter 8, he explains about having our minds set on the wrong nature of life, but if we have our mind set on what God's Spirit desires, we have life and peace. He gives this promise: "We know that in all things God works for the good of those who love him, who have been called according to his purpose" (8:28).

I can say from my own experience that if we are open to hearing and learning from God, we will get new insights. God's promise to work all things for good to those who love him is something we should all replay in our minds. Another insight from Paul is, "Do not conform any longer to the pattern of this world, but be transformed by the renewing of your mind" (Romans 12:2).

In the first chapter of his second letter, the apostle Peter wrote a very insightful comment to us about all the true and positive things God has given all of us. In verse 15, Peter promises he will make every effort to see that after his departure in life we will always remember these things. So as I memorize this concept I am aware of all the positives God has given me!

In my past I was on the wrong path when I got stuck on the negatives and kept replaying them. Then I took control of my reactions and feelings by developing the Event Wheel. I drew pictures of it on sticky notes and put them all around the house, even my bathroom mirror and on the dashboard in my car. You should do your best to replicate a simple version of the wheel for your personal life. I drew one that was very simple and just added the four words in the event wheel tool that I drew. It became immensely helpful as a visual tool to keep me on the narrow path and control my thoughts. Here's the tool:

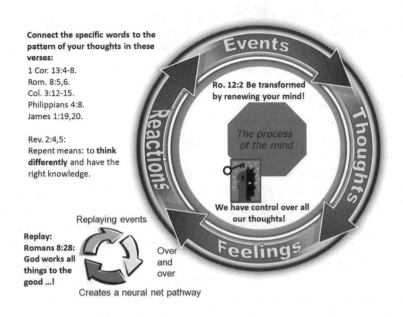

When I started controlling my thoughts and attitudes, then my feelings and reactions changed. Amazingly, my boss's reactions toward me improved when I got my thinking under control. The benefits were overwhelmingly positive. Things became clearer. I could now deal with any issue that came up, even bad things that happened at my job. I knew I could never find the perfect job or the perfect boss. But these good outcomes came because I processed through the problems and chose to become free of my negative thoughts and attitudes. When I got rid of them, my reactions changed toward others. I did not want to fix them; I wanted to fix myself.

My problems did not go away, but the way I handled them changed fundamentally. It all proved to me the truth of what Paul urged in Romans 12:2 when he told us not to "conform ... to the pattern of this world, but be transformed by the renewing of your mind."

Mentors and Disciples

I knew that spending a lot more time praying would be the most important thing I could do, so I prayed a lot. There are other key principles in the Bible about having mentors, being a disciple, discipling others, and confessing and admitting our problems daily. John 13:35 says, "By this all men will know that you are my disciples, if you love one another." And Matthew 28:19 says, "Therefore go and make disciples of all nations."

Such positive concepts help one deal with the negative things in life, so my pastor, Doug, and a few others hear from me and encourage me. I do the same for others. Discussing my struggles with thoughts and attitudes and telling my friends and mentor what I am doing wrong is more than just helpful; it's critical. Here's why: "Therefore confess your sins to each other and pray for each other so that you may be healed" (James 5:16).

Another key step in the process of change is to have others who can support us. This is part of God's plan. Being open to fellow Christians you know and trust is crucial. God is not visible to us in a physical way, but God working through his children is another story. So when we are stuck in a negative attitude, it is important to connect with friends and fellow Christians. It helps us in the process of change, and God becomes ever more tangible.

Doug and the others listened to me, prayed with me, and advised me in the Lord. Hebrews 3:13 says to "encourage one another daily, as long as it is called today, so that none of you may be hardened by sin's deceitfulness." The Bible is very clear about us daily confessing to, helping instruct, and encouraging one another.

When my friends reflected on what I shared, they saw some patterns. For example, it became obvious that what made me mad was not always something others had done to me, but that I had done to others. For me, this was a revelation. I started remembering all I had done or said, and it turned out that the things my bosses were doing to me were the things I did to others when I was a boss!

Now, instead of thinking negatively about my boss, I try to talk to him about things I struggle with. He gives me good feedback and valuable insights. So much so that I treat him and think of him as a friend. My current boss is a real friend!

I discovered I was like my bosses, and that I am quite capable of doing the very things to others that my bosses had done to me. I knew I had done things on the same scale, but I thought I had done them at a much lower level of intensity. I thought that on a scale of one to ten, their attacks were a nine or ten, whereas mine might have been a five to seven. As I thought about it, however, I realized that the people I had offended may have put my deeds on a higher scale than I had done to my bosses. This helped me let go of my judgment of them. I started forgiving my bosses—and appreciating how much they must have been struggling with their need for respect, honor, and significance, and to be seen as valuable employees.

Making My Bosses Look Good

A new objective arose when I began forgiving my bosses. As my attitude shifted from negative to positive, I wanted to help them look good. I found myself reacting less. Rather, I would listen to them carefully and reflect back what they said to be sure I understood them. I did this even when their words sounded mean or critical. The main thing was to understand their perspective and let them know I wanted to help. I also wanted them to know I appreciated them.

This new approach freed me from reactions and negative attitudes. And it took away my desire to ridicule my bosses or say negative things about them to others. I started telling people what I had learned about myself, and that I enjoyed working for my bosses regardless of how they treated me. I was experiencing a change within myself! I was far from being perfect, but I had no desire to stay on my negative path.

Even today when I experience a dustup with a boss, I can still be tempted to react and get stuck on negative thoughts. But I do that less and less. And usually, when I get stuck like that I quickly choose to stop thinking negatively and replay my new, more positive motives and thoughts. This new process allows me to stop being furious, judgmental, and controlling. My new goal is not about what I should or should not do; it is about putting behind me a judgmental and critical spirit.

Because of my new perspective, all of my bosses became comfortable and friendly with me. In my training sessions they began telling others positive things about me. When one of my bosses, who lived in another country, quit his job, he talked to me to find out when I would next be going to his country for a conference or convention. When I went, he and his wife took me out to dinner and hung out with me. He even invited me to go skiing with them and stay with them at a house they rented when they came to Colorado on a vacation. Here is the incredible part: This was the same man who caused the convention disaster at Las Vegas!

Something Else in Las Vegas

Another significant event happened in Las Vegas, this time at a training session. While I was handing out documents to the attendees, another boss said something that was critical about me. I had no idea what he meant or why he said it. The way the group reacted, it was obvious he was wrong. But I reacted to him in front of the group in an inappropriate way. I judged him and made him look stupid in front of everyone. I felt bad and realized I had just made things worse.

I had the group take a break so I could take ten minutes to refresh my mind about what I learned about replaying the good instead of the bad. Then I approached my boss, put my hand on his shoulder, looked in his eyes, and made it clear that I was not mad at him and that I was sorry for what both of us had experienced. The rest of the day we spent time in front of the group letting them know how much we appreciated each other.

Since I went through the process I have described, I love my job! Because I have control over how I process my thoughts, I am no longer attached to my old patterns. I have not been totally free of job problems, but in the past ten years all of my interactions with my bosses have been good and positive.

Big Ifs

A group of insights were very helpful during all of this. I call them the Big Ifs. These are the things I needed to consider and commit to doing to keep me on the right path:

- If bad things happen, I can stop replaying the negatives. Even if I start replaying the negatives, I can stop.
- If I am open-minded, there is more opportunity to discover why things sometimes do not work out.
- If I do not defend myself and make excuses, people do not generally react negatively to me.
- If I am willing to listen and consider others' experiences, I might learn things I never considered or experienced before.
- If I listen, I might gain more respect and improve relationships.
- If I reflect what was said to me—even if it is negative—it would start losing its accusative attitude.
- If I consider another person's point of view, it expands my potential for more knowledge.
- If I want to change but don't know how, I can listen to others and consider their advice—even if that advice is rude or wrong.
- If I stay connected to God, I will get thoughts that are real and way beyond my flesh.

There may be more Big Ifs, but those are certainly the obvious ones. It is easy to forget them, so I find that I need to keep them in mind daily. Now when I am replaying negative thoughts, I remember sooner rather than later to stop repeating the negatives. I also make fewer excuses about my problems and spend less time looking at everyone else's problems. Although negative events still trigger negative thoughts and reactions, I am more open to stepping into a neutral zone or remembering positive experiences and concepts.

My experience of change is about my relationship with God and staying connected to him and remembering critical concepts that many verses reveal. The Bible helps me see just how deeply the Lord loves his creation. I understand more and more about what God has done for me—and within me—and what my relationship to him should be. Here are some examples and portions of verses I memorize:

- Colossians 3:2: "Set your mind on things above, not on earthly things."
- Philippians 4:8: "Whatever is true, whatever is noble, whatever is right, whatever is pure, whatever is lovely, whatever is admirable—if anything is excellent or praiseworthy—think about such things."
- 1 Corinthian 13:4–8. Love is patient, love is kind. It does not envy. It does not boast. It is not proud, it is not rude, it is not self-seeking, it is not easily angered, it keeps no record of wrongs.
- 2 Corinthian 1:3, 4. Praise be to the God and Father of our Lord Jesus Christ, the father of compassion and the God of all comfort who comforts us in all our troubles, so that we can comfort those in any trouble with the comfort we ourselves have received from God.

Staying Connected

The Bible keeps me on the right path and helps me remember that "in all things God works for the good of those who love him, who have been called according to his purpose" (Rom. 8:28). Using the Event Wheel and the Narrow Path tools helps me remember to stand in the middle path without being passive or aggressive. It helps me shift my attitude from negative to positive, control my thoughts, replay positive thoughts and outcomes, look to mentors, and be a disciple of Christ.

When people read a Christian book they will come to a laid out passage of scripture and often they skip it, thinking the author is going to explain it while they keep reading. Even if they read it, most people won't remember it throughout the book. I wrote Romans 8:28 many times throughout the book for a very experiential outcome. I hope you will remember it for the rest of your life!

Here's why; Romans 8:28 is a critical verse to remember and replay in our minds every day. We can forget this: "in *all* things God works for the good ..." And it says "of those who love him ..." We can't possibly love God until we believe and remember how deeply loved we are by him. This verse had become a living reality to me in most of my stories because they all worked to the good when I believed and remembered how loved I was by God. Then I loved God and I was able to love others, including a moron in the Arches National Park story which is two stories after this one. But I had forgotten that verse for many years prior. When I forgot it, I was stuck on the wrong mental path and was worried, fearful or in a panic and could be angry or enraged.

I work through life issues almost weekly with a group of people: my daughter Kari, my son Ian, some others that are close friends and others who I know from Church. When they tell me problems, I repeat Romans 8:28 and they looked shocked. They realize they kept forgetting as the verse's truth dawns on them again. Romans 8:28 will become instinctual because *all* things God works to the good. Every time they have a problem, they focus on the problem and don't remember that God can turn it all to the good, if they love him. If they remember that God loves them deeply, they will love God and will be able to love others, because God's love is in them and all things work to the good! I trust you will love reading that verse every time in the book!

DREAM FROM
GOD

The root of my anger toward my wife, Debbie, was revealed about a year and a half before our divorce. This is my story about a true dream; you will realize what brought my heart changes.

On a Thursday evening my wife and I met with Doug and his wife Rebecca. They were counseling us about financial issues, and the counseling session was awkward and uncomfortable. From that night through Saturday, Deb and I continued arguing about money. This is what I wrote in my journal on Saturday morning:

> Deb and I have been fighting and it's been a disaster. I've been furious and feeling justified. I have been asking God why can't I show hurt instead of anger? I haven't gotten any answer yet.

I had an interesting dream that Saturday night, which I recorded in my journal on Sunday morning:

God woke me up, I thought. But I wasn't awake; I was having a dream. I started thinking about all that Deb has done in specific detail in the last day or so, and I asked myself, "How can she blame me or use me as her excuse for the way she treats me?" I then heard God ask me, "Why are you using her as your excuse for your anger?" I had no answer. I kept asking God, "How can she use me as her excuse?" Then God would ask me again why I used her as my excuse for anger. He didn't justify Debbie or make me feel defensive.

In response to this interaction this question came to my mind: "If Deb has no excuse to justify the way she treats me, and I won't let her use me as her excuse, why should I use her as mine?"

Then I went through this conversation all over again, but this time I was not having it with God. I was having it with my pastor, Doug, and his wife, Rebecca. I kept saying, "I don't care if I get my part fixed. How can she continue to get away with treating me like this and using me as her excuse?"

They wouldn't answer! Then God did. He said, "How can you continue to use Debbie as yours?"

So I went through each and every point of the issue, just like I did at the start, and told Doug and Rebecca how awful Debbie was and how I wasn't going to let her get off the hook by letting her use me as her excuse for anger. God would say, "Then how are you going to get off the hook using Debbie as your excuse for anger?"

God said repeatedly, "You have the *reasons* for anger, but not the *right*." He said, "These are the reasons you are angry, but what right do you have to be angry?"

I couldn't answer. I didn't have any right, and I couldn't get a clear picture of how to answer God. Together we went through both sets of concepts again. God asked, "What right?" and I would answer with, "The reason."

After going through it all with no understanding, God put me back to sleep and gave me another dream. (This is the part that's odd. I thought I was awake, but I wasn't.)

In the extra dream I went to a restaurant in Delta, Colorado, for a meal. My wife and I used to eat there a lot when we lived in Cedaredge. While I was there, the manager treated me shamelessly. I don't remember why he treated me this way, but I went through a complete dining experience with this total jerk of a manager. He blew it with me over and over. He got angry at me and blamed me for something, and then finally I left the restaurant.

Someone saw the whole exchange between the manager and me, and they contacted the owner of the restaurant—who turned out to be Bob Young. (Bob Young is the owner and founder of Alpine Banks in Western Colorado, one of the most successful privately owned banking systems in the United States.) He doesn't know me well, though we have met a number of times.

Bob somehow found me at the restaurant while I was leaving and put me in his car and took care of me. He listened to my story, comforted me, took my side, and couldn't believe his manager had treated me so shamelessly. He told me he couldn't justify his manager's action because he had never given him the authority or the right to be angry at the customers. He repeated several times that this manager had not gotten Bob's authority to be rude and angry.

Bob did something to make me feel really special and completely erased any bad feelings: He let me know how important I was and how much he appreciated me as his customer, and how badly he felt that his representative had abused his authority. I remember thinking in the dream that I felt very special that Bob valued me so much.

Then I woke up. (I didn't really—it was all part of the dream.) I now understood the meaning of God's question: "What right do you have to be angry?"

Next I got a vision of a guy who was stuck out in the boondocks with no vehicle, so he stole an eighteen-wheeler to get where he was going. Then he got pulled over by a cop. He was very polite to the cop and explained his reason for needing a ride to get somewhere and why he stole the truck. The cop understood his problem, but said the guy had no right or authority or license to drive an eighteen-wheeler—especially someone else's. He couldn't be safe driving one because he was not trained to drive a truck that big.

Then I asked God why all of this applies to me. God said, "I didn't give you authority to use anger, and you have no right to use it. You are not trained, and you don't know when or how to use anger correctly. You don't have my permission to use your reasons as a right to be angry. You couldn't use anger properly. As God, I judge others correctly, but you don't have the right to be angry at Debbie. I only gave you the right and permission to love, cherish, and take care of my daughter, just as the restaurant manager only had the owner's permission to care for Bob's customers."

It made sense. In the dream, I realized that it did not matter that the man in my dream needed to get where he was going. If a person cannot safely drive an eighteen-wheeler, and if it is against the law for someone to drive one without training and practice, then driving it would be potentially deadly.

I didn't hear any of this dream as a personal slam from God. But it was just a clear illustration of why this question in the book of Jonah is so valid: "But the Lord replied, 'Have you any right to be angry?'" (4:4).

Then I got a vision of Jonah and the vine and why God used that as an illustration in the book's fourth chapter:

> Then the Lord God provided a vine and made it grow up over Jonah to give shade for his head to ease his discomfort, and Jonah was very happy about the vine. But at dawn the next day God provided a worm, which chewed the vine so that it withered. When the sun rose, God provided a scorching east wind, and the sun blazed on Jonah's head so that he grew faint. He wanted to die, and said, "It would be better for me to die than to live."
>
> But God said to Jonah, "Do you have a right to be angry about the vine?"
>
> "I do," he said. "I am angry enough to die."
>
> But the Lord said, "You have been concerned about this vine, though you did not tend it or make it grow. It sprang up overnight and died overnight. But Nineveh has more than a hundred and twenty thousand people who cannot tell their right hand from their left, and many cattle as well. Should I not be concerned about that great city?"
>
> —Jonah 4:6–12

The details of my dream were the same as the details in the story of Jonah. I received insight that God has cared for Debbie's problems and is tending her, just as he did when he showed concern for the people of Nineveh. At times she doesn't necessarily know her right hand from her left. But shouldn't God be concerned for her? He knows her problems, so I don't have to be angry over them. Isn't it better that he care about her needs than that he give me the right to be angry at her about her problems?

This whole time God was walking me through and clarifying the root of my anger toward Debbie. The way God teaches, I didn't have to feel dirty, guilty, or humiliated. His teaching gave me a clear picture. I felt really special that God was willing to walk me through this and give me clarity and a sense of the truth of things. This is where the dream ended.

Now I Get It!

When I really woke up the next morning, I wrote the details of the dream in my journal, then I wrote another portion as a summation. Here is what became very clear from the whole dream: God has given me authority and permission to take care of his daughter, not to be angry at her for her faults. I picked Debbie to be my wife, so it is my responsibility to take care of her. Taking care of her is all I have a right to do. If she has any issues of anger, God will take care of any judgment, not me. I couldn't possibly find the right way to be angry. My anger doesn't do anything to help others or solve issues. I may feel hurt and angry, but I don't have a right to use my anger. I haven't been given divine authority to judge and control others, so I need to quit walking around feeling justified because my wife uses me as her excuse to get angry. If all that is true, how can I use Debbie as my excuse?

A change took place in my life, and I started on a very different path with my attitude toward my wife. My anger hadn't vanished, but it was disappearing and I could see that change was becoming real. The proof of this came the day after the dream. My wife assaulted me verbally, and she was as far off track as I had ever seen. Yet instead of getting angry, I felt hurt—which was a very different feeling. I told her about the hurt and said I couldn't keep talking to her and needed to walk away for a bit. She came and found me and apologized. We wound up having one of the most positive and productive talks about our anger and our pattern of dealing with each other. It went over so well, we were actually laughing out loud.

I discerned many insights from this dream. I certainly couldn't have come up with them on my own, and for months as I replayed the dream in my mind, it freed me from needing to use my anger to deal with issues. This was proof again that God would continue to heal me.

Weeks later, Debbie was doing something with money that was way out of bounds. I talked calmly to her about the problem. She was irritated at me, but did not act in any hostile way. I let her know she was loved, but that regardless of the love I had for her, the money could not be spent the way she was planning. She was definitely miffed with me. I just absorbed it and had no reaction toward her. Within a half hour, she was very pleased with me and was being affectionate.

More Proof

When Debbie started the divorce, she triggered a number of bad financial problems. In fact, the money situation went haywire. I was tempted to go into a rage, but I didn't. I did not want to use my anger anymore, though the things that happened might have given me justification. But I think God had gotten to the root of my anger and healed me of it. I wasn't simply pretending my anger was gone; it really was gone. In the midst of some horrible events, my anger did not take over my personality.

As the divorce continued, there were more financial disasters. I didn't handle them all perfectly, but I could not stay angry for very long. I actually found myself repulsed when I experienced anger. I replayed the dream and remembered how good it felt when I was not controlled by my emotions. I just let go of anger, and it was no longer in control of me.

Prior to the Dream

Anger toward my wife was my biggest long-term problem; it took me years to work through it. Eventually I took responsibility for my anger, but that wasn't the only positive change I needed to experience. It was a piece of the puzzle, but not the whole solution. I also had anger toward others and life in general, and in my mind this anger was justified. But over time I decided I'd had enough. I finally wanted real change—and realized that my anger had to be conquered. Some of the things that triggered and fueled my anger were clear. Others were not.

I found that change is a process. Change from the inside was evident to me (and others) concerning my work life and my relationship with the kids. But the biggest problem between my wife and me was money.

I would go from rage to complete disinterest, then back to rage. I swung between both extremes. I couldn't find the center. I would scream, yell, cuss, and holler—or sometimes I would just walk off and say, "Screw it. I am done with this." But I could not ignore it. I was stewing on it in my mind and could not let go. I remember telling Doug about my reactions showing both extremes. As he would reflect them back, it was obvious I was not "fixed." I still needed healing from the inside out.

It has been more than a decade since the root of my anger began changing. Today I live in comfort, peace, and real joy about what has happened with my anger issue. I am not perfect, and I never will be, but it is encouraging when I experience things going wrong around me and I am able to stand in the situation. I want to live without judging people and instead love others unconditionally. I no longer wish to use anger, and I love the freedom from my old self. It is one of the best experiences in my life to be free of my old style. This allows me to focus on standing in the narrow life path and stepping into the chaos. The next story will reveal these concepts even deeper and prove there is even more freedom.

A MORON AT ARCHES NATIONAL PARK SHOVES CHANGES DOWN MY THROAT

Arches National Park is a beautiful place. When I got there on a Wednesday in the first week in November, I had the whole campground to myself. I arrived at just the right time to experience one of the most spectacular sunsets I had seen in forty years of camping. But I started experiencing something embarrassing, so I was glad no one was around. I was climbing in the middle of an arch as the sun set. The rocks around me looked like they were on fire. (See the photo in the back of the book.) Amazed at the beauty I saw happening around me, I sat on a boulder and wept out loud, I had never done that before, and I was afraid someone would hear me and start laughing.

One reason I took this vacation, planning to be alone for a portion of it, was to spend time pondering, writing, praying, and listening to God about how a church elder meeting negatively impacted me and how I might experience a change in my heart. I was accused of not having what it takes to provide good ideas about using the new gathering center we had just built for the community. Their comments were controlling me in a very bad way. I had been working through them for the last six months, but had not gotten free of my negative thoughts about myself from two people's specific comments.

That first night at Arches I reread the first chapter in the book of Colossians and stewed on the concept that because of Christ's death, we are free from blemish and accusation. The apostle Paul writes that God "has rescued us from the dominion of darkness and brought us into the kingdom of the Son he loves, in whom we have redemption, the forgiveness of sins" (1:13–14). Then Paul writes this:

> Once you were alienated from God and were enemies in your minds because of your evil behavior. But now he has reconciled you by Christ's physical body through death to present you holy in his sight, without blemish and free from accusation—if you continue in your faith, established and firm, not moved from the hope held out in the gospel.
>
> —Colossians 1:21–23

Normally, accusations send my emotions down the toilet. I get angry, fearful, and judgmental—especially toward myself. Am I stupid? Don't I have what it takes? Don't I bring anything to the table? Those are the kinds of questions I ask myself when I am accused.

I wrote some verses from Colossians chapter one on an index card and stuck it in my pocket. I planned to take a long hike the next day and ponder them. I use the card as a tool in memorizing Scripture. As a habit, I memorize the Bible by repeating verses out loud when I hike. This makes me feel like I am hiking with God (which I am), and it is an encouraging experience. This time, hiking and climbing proved as emotional as the dramatic sunset, but it was not fun. Well, not the whole time.

I was still the only person in the campground when I started out at about 11:00 A.M. I wandered all over the place and found some arches and great rock formations with beautiful views. Miles away across a large valley, I saw a ridgeline of very bizarre rocks. I decided to head that way. The distance didn't bother me because I planned to be in this wilderness all day. As I was wandering toward the ridge, I was repeating Scripture verses and talking aloud to God about the concept of being free of accusation in my struggles with myself and others. I wanted to hear from God and have him reveal what was keeping me stuck.

A Moron Shows Up

I felt like God had given me the whole park to myself. It was like playing in God's backyard. As I experienced all the beauty around me, I felt loved and close to the Creator The thought occurred to me that God creates not only for his delight, but also for ours. And I was walking with him in his creation.

As that thought came to me, I saw someone off in the distance coming down the valley at a perpendicular angle to me. I kept heading toward the ridge. After about ten minutes it seemed obvious he and I would cross paths within yards of each other.

This was the only other person I had seen in the whole place. I smiled as I thought of saying hi and making some comment about this incredible park. Within minutes we would cross each other's path. As I was about to cross the trail he was on, I said, "Hi, how's it going?"

He yelled at me in disgust. "What the hell are you doing? You're ruining the soil! You can't just walk around here any way you want. You need to get on the trail."

I looked away from him and walked right past.

Then he yelled, "You're breaking the law, you jerk! I hope you wind up in jail."

I walked a bit faster, and my mind started to reel. Smoke probably came out of my ears. This moron dumped on me verbally, and I was no longer a happy camper. In my mind I was fuming and yelling, and some vile things came out of my mouth.

Name-Calling

I thought of many names I could call him, but they mostly stayed in my mind. I was stunned at what just happened, and the negative thoughts were coming so fast, I couldn't stop them. I tried to grab hold of myself and asked God to help me get through this. I tried to forgive the man, but every time I did, the same names came right back to mind. Talk about being accused and affected in a bad way.

I started to realize something. Often when I got accused, there were foul thoughts and names I called others that instantly sprang to mind. This guy had just called me a jerk, and because he was a big man I thought he would jump on me and beat the crap out of me if he knew what I was thinking about him. At a recent meeting at church, two people said some inappropriate things to me, and after the meeting the same mental process had gone on in my mind. As I thought of the meeting, it was clear that the two people had reacted outwardly. But my reaction was worse because mine was internal. Outwardly I looked like everything was fine, but inwardly my mind was racing with unsuitable thoughts.

At that meeting after their negative comments, I had even said some positive things. My friend Doug was there, and he told me it was evident that something was going on inside me. He told me to ponder it all, and that was why I had come to this park—for a private vacation to process the concept of accusations.

But as with the meeting at church, I could not get the bad thoughts to stop. I tried forgiving this moron, but that seemed way beyond my capabilities. I was now about a mile from him, and I could see him walking down the valley. I was headed to the ridge and I was starting to climb it. Once I got on top, the view was overwhelming. As I looked down the valley, I saw a huge arch—and I saw that moron heading to it.

I knew I was going there also, but I wouldn't do it while that guy was there. I got a thought: I could run back to his car in some parking lot and throw a rock through his windshield! I had some even worse thoughts, too.

Maybe There Were Some Signs

Then I realized this event was not a coincidence! This matter of accusations was exactly what I had been asking God to teach me about. The more I thought of this, the more I was shocked and amused. I started laughing. I couldn't make this stuff up. Here in the middle of the wilderness, while talking out loud to God about why I am not free of accusations, I cross the path of someone I don't know, who assaults me with a nasty accusation! I am in God's backyard enjoying my time with him, and wham! I get hit with an accusation right between the eyes. Pretty funny.

Then it became clear what I was doing in my mind to this man. He was God's child, too. I had no right to think such things about him. My thoughts were an attack on part of God's creation.

For the rest of the day I looked for God to reveal things. I started hiking down the ridgeline and headed toward the big arch. (It is pictured in the back of the book also.) There were two people sitting at the bottom of the arch, and I asked them if they had seen the other fellow. They said he had gone on the trail ahead and was heading back up the valley. Whew, I missed him!

While I was hiking, more things went through my mind. I told myself that the way I had been hiking was perfectly fine. After all, I had no idea about any hiking rules in the park. Then I thought I may have missed some signs about certain rules, and I made sure I was walking on rocks and in little dry washes.

I didn't mind doing that, but what was going on in my head was strange. I was trying to convince myself that I had done that the whole time I had been wandering all over the national park. But in truth it had never occurred to me to stay on the rocks, stay in washes, or even walk on trails. I even took a picture of my footprints across a virgin sand hill beneath an arch. I couldn't wait to put my footprints on this hillside under an arch and take a photo of them. Maybe I was breaking some law; maybe I was a jerk. I was starting to feel guilt.

As I continued hiking I became more nervous about where I was walking. In my mind I was trying to make myself look like a hero and a tree-hugger, and prove my innocence of the other hiker's accusations. The exposure of all the B.S. bad stuff going on in my head was real. I got past the nervousness and realized there probably were some rules about hiking, and I did not know them. It was also clear that no one could always stay on a trail, but that walking in a dry wash and staying on rocks made sense. I realized I would have to be prudent about where I walked and how I did it. I thought that if I could just get past my lack of expertise, I would continue to enjoy the hike.

When I started hiking more carefully, I began accusing the other hiker in my mind. How dare he speak to me that way. I am God's child, and I am walking in my Father's park. It is not *his* Father's park—it is *my* Father's park. My hike was much more significant than his because I had been out talking to God and was being spiritual. And I was a good guy! How did he have any right to accuse me?

Now it occurred to me that I was being just like my accuser. I was so stuck on seeing things my way, I could not let go. My hike was turning into a mental wrestling match. And I couldn't stop either his mental assault or my own.

As I came over another set of rock formations, I saw three more arches and headed to them. When I got there, I asked God to show me why I had been struggling so much in the last three hours, and what was keeping me stuck in this pattern.

While standing there, I got the insight that God was going to show me what I need to know. This whole event was orchestrated for my healing. That put a smile on my face, and I didn't have a single bad thought for the rest of my hike.

I got back to camp and took a shower, started a campfire, and sat down and listened to Carlos Nakai's desert flute music, great background for watching the sunset. I could not stop laughing out loud at what the day had been like. I grilled a steak and had a great night. When I went to bed, I knew I had not gotten the complete answer to my problem, but I was at peace that it would come.

A New Trail

When I got up the next morning, things were much clearer. I understood why the hike had been such a mental wrestling match. I saw the connection between what happened on the hike and all the other times I have been accused. I had thought the same thing about work, bosses, people at church, and anyone else who didn't meet my expectations.

When I fall short of meeting the expectations of others, like the guy on the trail, and there are any accusations, it drains my heart of the four basic needs we all have. (These are being loved and loving others, self-worth, significance, and security.)

Many stories in the Old Testament are filled with the promise of these four concepts. God promised to make his children be loved, and he wanted them to love all others. He committed to their value as his children, and he told them things to do that would prove their self-worth from God's perspective. He told them the things to do that would provide real significance for their lives and for others'. And God provided security with promises of protection and provisions, as well as the things they needed to make their life secure.

The evidence that I had lost those needs was the fact that I had been hiding somewhere on the trail, afraid the moron would beat me up—clearly a security issue. There was no love lost between us, so the need about love was gone. He obviously did not think I had any worth, and my self-worth was at an all-time low. From his perspective, what I was doing had no real importance, so he saw me as insignificant.

I in turn had tried to refill my heart using all those thoughts, reactions, excuses, and justifications—whatever it took to get my needs refilled. The reason why God does not—and will not—accuse us became very clear. He does not want to drain our hearts; he wants to fill them. Accusations pull the plug in our hearts and drain us of our basic needs. God will not accuse us. That is the promise from Colossians 1:22! "But now he has reconciled you by Christ's physical body through death to present you holy in his sight, without blemish and free from accusation."

God used the event at Arches National Park to give me some discernment into my problem with accusations. I had put this man's assessment of me between me and God. I hadn't realized that a deep wound had been inflicted on me in the past and that it was now holding me captive. I had believed at some level for many years that others' accusations of me were more believable than God's unconditional love.

The Bible expounds the concept of God's love, and I had gotten it intellectually—as head knowledge. But after running into that accuser in the desert, I realized the idea of divine love had not penetrated my heart. Though I fought against the man's accusations, in reality I accepted the idea that I was a loser. I spent three hours wrestling against that, but I could not stop it. I accepted his accusation, as I had accepted most accusations against me for most of my life. But until now I had not grasped that believing what others said about me caused me to put something between me and God. That was idolatry.

All this time I had been trying to look good to everyone so I could have my needs met. I expected people to love me the way I needed to be loved. God has used the last six months, as I have had people expose my unsuitable thoughts, to prove this to me. Though I was angry or hurt and thought better of myself, I still felt I needed to feel approved and respected by the ones who wounded me. I had believed God's love intellectually, but not practically.

That next morning at camp, I realized I needed to hike a new trail. I can choose to remember and replay in my thoughts what is true about God's love for me. I can stand in faith that he will provide it no matter what happens He has promised to turn all things to the good: "We know that in all things God works for the good of those who love him, who have been called according to his purpose" (Rom. 8:28). And he will never blame me.

Humility is Not an Ornament

The next morning I was up at sunrise, having a cup of coffee, and listening to Christian recording artist John Michael Talbot while writing the story of the previous day. I could not stop smiling. I was once again enjoying the adventure of my life. I am so grateful to the Lord for all he has done for me. I am grateful for all the experiences he has given me. I am comfortable about what I experienced at the national park—that I am getting freer of my old self. Freedom is the word I use about my life, and I love being free. *I am free!*

I am at a point in life where I usually want the opinions of others. I am more committed to pondering what others think about me than I am about defending myself. I could not have come to that point until I understood the truth about forgiveness and God's love—and I experienced it personally. This episode in the park taught me that pride and arrogance can be exposed, and that humility is a behavior that can be controlled. Humility is not an ornament I can hang on myself. It is a real decision of the heart.

It's great to have good friends to help you. But with trust and faith, no matter who assaults or rejects you, God can use any opportunity for your good. He can even use hikers who accost others in parks. It took all of these experiences over the past six months for me to become open to hearing from God. When I did, these are some of the things I learned:

- I must never forget the stories in my life that teach me of God's love for all of his children.
- I need to connect God's love for me to my life on a daily basis.
- I need to keep focused and remember the verse that I am free of accusation from God. He sees me without blemish, and I am dearly loved. I need to remember that while others will not fill my needs, God will.
- I need to remember there is not a single person who can love as perfectly as God. Only God can fill the four basic needs of our hearts: loving others and being loved, self-worth, significance, and security.
- I need to stop letting accusations curtail my spirit and my life.
- I need to remember that on the aggressive side of my personality, accusations cause constant battling within me, and they trigger anger, a judgmental attitude, hate, and disgust.
- I need to remember that on the passive side of my personality, accusations cause fear, avoidance, insecurity, and worry.
- I need to remember that while outward events trigger the emotions, the root of the problem causes bad feelings to stay within me and creates deep wounds.

I tell this story to show how God revealed my root problem. I believe I am on a path toward healing. I have been accused since that hiking trip, and the results have been mixed. Sometimes my reaction is minimal; at other times it comes and tempts me. But when I remember the positives and let go of the negatives, things seem to go my way. It requires keeping an open mind and staying connected to God—during good times and bad.

The Title of the Book

Although it was not her intention, my mother provided the title for this book. On a Memorial Day weekend, I was driving to Arizona to see my daughter for the first time in more than two years since the divorce. I hoped it would be an opportunity to improve our relationship. I had not spoken to Kari, even by phone, because I was honoring her request for me not to contact her. We were supposed to meet for lunch in Yuma, Arizona, on a Sunday. I drove sixteen hours to get there. My mother and daughter lived in the same town and were in periodic contact with each other. My son Ian was living with me, but he stayed in touch with his sister and grandmother. He helped coordinate with my mother the arrangements for me to meet Kari.

Mom was full of good intentions for me and my daughter, so she was very open to arranging our lunch meeting. I did not want her to put any pressure on Kari, though Mom thought the meeting was critical for my daughter to talk to me and get reconnected to her dad. Mom had been hurting for me because my loss of relationship with Kari had gone on for years. When I left my mom on my fourteenth birthday, I did not talk to her for years! So it made sense why she was so passionate to put the two of us together. I had discussed my concern with her a few times, and I told Mom I wanted the meeting to happen naturally and that it should be based on Kari's choice. I felt it was critical that my daughter make her own decision, without any pressure, on whether to see me.

I arrived late in the afternoon on Friday, hopeful my daughter and I would meet for lunch on Sunday. I had to return to Colorado on Monday, which was Memorial Day. Mom called my daughter on Friday to remind her about getting together with me. Kari was not home, so Mom left a message.

That evening we had not heard from my daughter. Mom was concerned and called her several times and left a message each time. After four or five tries, I told her not to call anymore. She seemed disappointed that I was being nonchalant about the situation.

I told her this was not about me getting my needs met, but about my daughter's concerns. We had to honor her feelings, regardless of how much we both wanted it to work out.

That Saturday evening my son-in-law, Jason, called. Mom answered the phone. I had never met nor talked to my son-in-law. I heard Mom talking to him, and it was clear something was going on medically with my new grandson (whom I had also never seen). That was why Kari had not returned the calls.

My mother tried to encourage my son-in-law to talk to me. She was doing everything in her power for my sake. My heart sank when I heard Mom pushing and trying to control Jason, and I knew she had crossed the line with him. He hung up on her. I did not get to talk to him or see my daughter and grandson until after another year of waiting and hoping.

Mom came out of the bedroom, where she had been on the phone, brokenhearted and teary-eyed. We had a lengthy and candid discussion. My mom was hurt deeply, and she was embarrassed that she could not help.

I felt I had walked the narrow path and was prepared to handle things exactly as I did. I had faith that God would still turn all things to the good! God had truly brought about a change in me. I did not have any thoughts of anger toward my mother or daughter. Instead

I had peace that I had done what needed to be done and that I was who'I needed to be. I had my daughter's best interest at heart, and I didn't need to know all her reasons for not meeting me.

Perhaps the trip was more important for my mother than for either me or my daughter. I had been tested once again as to my motives toward others, and all the way home I was satisfied and joyful that I had been so free of my old patterns.

As I drove home I called Doug to tell him about the event. Somewhere in the story I said, "My mother was blinded by good intentions."

He said, "It sounds like the title of a book you should write."

He was right. I realized most of my failures in life, including my part in the divorce and the consequences of forty-plus years, were often because I had also been blinded by good intentions.

I e-mailed Mom to ask her if she would be comfortable with me telling others this story. This is her reply:

Ah! I remember it all too well. You nailed it. You were happy as a clam. I was heartbroken and thought you had also lost your mind. I could not believe Jason hung up, and it was all because of my big mouth. One of Dick's favorite Scriptures for me was Proverbs 10:19: "When words are many, sin is not absent, but he who holds his tongue is wise." In other words, turn off the flow (a rather loose translation). I keep putting my foot in my mouth. The other was Psalm 141:3: "Set a guard over my mouth, O Lord; keep watch over the door of my lips." Not a Memorial Day passes that it does not come to mind.

Now I see through the dark mirror more clearly. Yes, you absolutely can use this in your memoir, and hopefully there may be something where I say something profound or wise....

As I am only seventy-five, going on fifty-seven; there may not be enough years left to do the wise-woman thing. Well, as William said in *Finding Forrester*, don't forget to write! May you continue to do the same. God bless, my love, Mom.

THE VALUE OF A SON COMPARED TO A FRYING PAN

I am in the middle of a mental battle. It fills my mind and heart. I know if I stay on the path of my negative thoughts, I will have an even bigger problem than the one I have struggled with for almost a half hour. So I am working through it and trying to find a more neutral path. I decided to start writing about it in my journal. Here is what I wrote:

Negative thoughts are coming at me repeatedly. I had a bad dream last night, and when I got up this morning the impact of that dream was in my face. The thoughts during the dream were very negative, and I was replaying them this morning while cooking breakfast. Aside from the dream, when I looked at the pans I was using to make eggs and pancakes, they were a mess. This annoyed me, and it became a battle in my mind that lasted for about half an hour.

I kept thinking that my pans were such a filthy mess that they are ruined. They had food stuck on them, and they looked like they had not been cleaned for months. (My son is the one who is supposed to clean them.) They were scratched and the Teflon had almost all been removed. The eggs weren't sliding and flipping the way I wanted them to, and neither were the pancakes. This brought me negative thoughts that made me angrier and angrier.

This is the worst part: Each negative thought had some truth, but I started adding an exaggeration to them. They became more negative and less accurate and were making me angrier.

Frying Pans Versus Ian

The pans were really not ruined, not even the ones that were damaged. My negative thoughts caused exaggeration. And when negative thoughts are overemphasized, that can put one on a downhill slide and trigger even more negative thoughts. Here is a silly example of such a progression: "My eggs and potatoes don't look the way I want them to look, and they won't taste good." That can lead to the next thought: "When my son moves out of the house, I will give him these pans. He will ask why I am giving them to him, and I will say it is because he ruined them. Why should I keep them?" Those actually were my thoughts that morning, and I was replaying them in my mind.

As I battled these thoughts, it occurred to me that I was judging Ian and that my anger and judgment could keep me stuck on the wrong path. I knew I had the ability to control my thoughts, and I did not want to get stuck in my old pattern of letting negative thoughts control me and damage my relationship with my son.

I began battling those thoughts and stopped replaying them. Then I recalled some specific, positive reasons my son was living with me. My priority was to have my son know that I loved him. Here are the thoughts I chose to remember:

- Lousy frying pans, or any other physical things, mean nothing to me compared to my son.
- I do not want to add to my son's life negative thoughts that might bring more frustration, guilt, and shame.
- I never want Ian to think he doesn't measure up to my expectations. That would only make things worse.
- I don't want to fix his symptoms in order to make me more comfortable. Let me fix myself first.

- I want to see his heart healed—not necessarily his symptoms and conduct.

As I replayed those thoughts in my mind, I lost my anger and was glad I had not let myself surrender to hostile thinking. I might remind my son to be more careful washing the pots and pans, but that is a far cry from accusing him of ruining things.

After writing in my journal what I was struggling with, I started to get on that narrow path. Writing helps me gain a new perspective after I've written about negative thoughts, feelings, and reactions. And when I write about positive things, that helps me remember them.

Sword Fighting for My Son

Learning to use positive thoughts as a weapon in the battle for the mind is like sword fighting. Negative thoughts come at me like sword thrusts from an enemy. Either I defend myself with positive thoughts as my sword, or I get cut and wounded as my negative thoughts are used by my enemy.

When I use positive thoughts, the enemy (my human nature) may try a couple more thrusts with negative thoughts. But because I have control over my thoughts, the negative attitude starts to go away and I experience real pleasure for having battled for my son's heart. My new positive thoughts overpowered the negatives!

The apostle Paul's second letter to the Corinthians tells us how and why this works: "For though we live in the world, we do not wage war as the world does. The weapons we fight with are not the weapons of the world. On the contrary, they have divine power to demolish strongholds. We demolish arguments and every pretension that sets itself up against the knowledge of God, and we take captive every thought to make it obedient to Christ" (10:3–5).

Had I battled for my own heart needs instead of my son's, I would have attacked him about his problems and tried to get him to meet my expectations. I would have tried to control and motivate him for my personal comfort. Then I would want to fix him for my convenience.

Though it would be helpful for my son to learn to improve in several areas, I cannot react negatively and accuse him, because that would cause him to do the same to me. The whole situation would get worse. His wounds would go deeper, and he would not experience the real reason I want him to live with me—for him to experience how much I love him.

The battle is real. If my interest in having my needs met overrides my responsibility to meet the needs of others, everyone loses. To battle rightly requires a decision of my will, and I can control that decision. It is a choice I now want to make because I have done things the wrong way for most of my life. I don't want to do that anymore. My decision over whose needs are served is not triggered by my feelings; it is a choice over which I have control.

Choosing to favor another's priorities does not necessarily have to do with one's feelings. It is mostly a commitment to love and to battle against the flesh. My emotional peace will come eventually, but at the start of the battle, getting the positive emotion is not the motivating factor.

Saving my son's heart and proving he is loved became my motive, but that motive would fall by the wayside if I keep repeating negative thoughts and forgetting the positive ones. When a negative reaction is my next step, another bad event happens. Now that I understand that, I don't want to react negatively.

I woke up the next morning and used my memory about positive things as armor to protect me and my son. But that lasted only about a day. When I got up the following morning, the living room was messy. The negative thoughts (sword thrust) started again, so I immediately began replaying the specific positive reasons my son was living with me. The bad thoughts vaporized and I sat in peace, knowing why I fight for my son's heart.

The day before I had thought about how I might address some of these things with my son. I envisioned simply asking him to do this or that differently, and I truly had no negative feelings about him. I was at peace and it seemed a very acceptable way to approach him. I did not expect he would keep doing things the way I wanted, but if that turned out to be true. I would not have been irritated. But I put my plan to speak to him aside and assumed I would address those things when the right opportunity came.

I saw Ian three times during the day, but there was no opportunity to bring up the request without interrupting what he was doing. Later that evening I considered this further. I realized I had already made these same requests several times over the last two years, including once in the last three months. This told me that my son's lifestyle is what it is. None of us—including my son—can change our behaviors until we have a heart change. And that is why I fight for his heart!

As I considered his possible reasons for being messy around the house, I was sure of one thing: He does not want to disobey or ignore me. I believe his lifestyle is a result of his brokenness, frustration, self-loathing, and his need to focus on making his life work. Those thoughts can preoccupy him, and they will continue to do so until he finds a way out. He may already realize he isn't doing things the way I would like, but he may have no energy to correct things. I don't read any of this as rebellion. I think he is struggling with life, like I did.

His needs for being loved and loving others, self-worth, significance, and security are possibly drained, and he may be spending time and energy focused on filling his needs. Or he might feel defeated and think there is little used in trying harder. Maybe he has no positive motivations! He is in the same boat I was in when he was younger.

As I thought things through, I had no sense of guilt about reminding him of what chores I would appreciate him doing around the house. I could ask him these things without replaying a bad attitude. But reminding him that he is not meeting my expectations might create an additional sense of failure. If he thinks he doesn't meet my expectations, he could feel he doesn't measure up to who he should be—and that would drain his basic needs even further. I do not want my son to think he is inadequate to fulfill my simple expectations.

This situation with my son teaches me that my negative thoughts are not likely to be accurate, because they are driven by negative perspectives. When I choose to let go of my negative thoughts, I realize over time that they are never completely correct. Most often they are not even near the ballpark. So I have learned that I can reconsider what I want to think about and come up with thoughts that are neutral or positive. The results are always surprising, because the new thoughts have the potential to put me into a middle path where I won't be aggressive or passive. This is the avenue that brings about wisdom and compassion, not the negative thoughts I was sure were right!

My .44 Magnum Will Fix My Pan

The real events and motives in my son's life are very different than what I expected. I am realizing that when I react to negative events, my thoughts are not helpful or accurate. The solution is to change my perspectives and motives. Then I am not wrestling with a flight or fight situation within myself—at least not at the level I used to.

I am not under pressure to get Ian to do what I want, nor do I fear asking because it will tick him off. I am standing in the heart-path of a battlefield for my son's life. I stand here by choice of my will and out of love for my son. I don't need my personal things protected for me to be at peace, full of joy, and deeply in love with my son. Today as I write this, my living room and kitchen are messy. Still, I am at peace. The Event Wheel from an earlier chapter really works.

I hope my son will go camping with me soon. I have taken the large, messed-up Teflon pan and put it in my camper. I want to tell him this story at camp and demonstrate that compared to him, my pan means nothing to me. I want to take the pan and set it out in the dirt or hang it from a tree and shoot it with my .44 Magnum. Then I would hand him a new pan and tell him to enjoy using it! With that positive attitude, I am a freer man to battle for my son. I am free from my old self, which was focused on my needs and my comfort. I am not perfect, and I may still screw up things, but I am different.

Dads Fighting for their Children

If I ever write another book, it will be on the fight for our children's hearts. Fighting for their hearts is not what I thought it would be like when I first had children. It is far more positive than I ever imagined.

Much of what I envisioned about influencing my children, protecting their hearts, and being the father I should be did not work out the way I expected. As I have told my stories to other dads, many admit they have been on a similar path of failure.

We all start out wanting to be great dads and heroes. I thought being a great dad meant having the right intentions, telling my kids what not to do, then telling them what to do and how to do it. Back then I used a lot of expectations, pressure, and all the other negative things I have written about.

I am so fortunate to have been given a new opportunity. I have my son living at home with me again, and it is just the two of us. He is now twenty-seven and has been with me four years. I have a new opportunity to be the dad I always wanted to be. This time around, I have the experience of knowing I am loved by God and having more wisdom about life. Because God fills my needs, I do not need my son to fill them. I have also forgiven the wounds caused by others. All this makes me a much freer man—free of my sinful human nature and free to be at peace with myself and at odds with my old negative perspectives.

My Life and My Son's Life

Prior to my son coming back home to live with me, he was living in Florida and struggling deeply. He was at the end of his rope, unable to make anything work out. He was very depressed. He told me some of the things he had experienced and what he was thinking about doing with his life. Much of it terrified me.

Ian said he was experiencing horrible events and terror with a drug dealer. Florida was the third place he had lived since moving from our home after the divorce. Prior to locating in Florida, he had lived in Denver and Phoenix, both of which were disastrous for him. When Ian left for Florida, he had nothing to take with him. He had lost everything he owned: his TV, all his furniture, and even most of his clothes. The only way he could get to Florida was by bumming a ride from someone he knew who was driving there. The driver told him he could not take anything with him, except a few days' worth of clothes. Ian drastically wanted and needed a life change, and that was the reason he left so quickly and let go of everything and everyone.

He had no money in Florida, not even the money to pay for the drugs he used. This became a serious issue with a major drug dealer. Ian had been there for many months and was stuck financially. Though he wanted to, he could not leave the state. He also knew that if he left Florida and hadn't squared things with the drug dealer, he would be hunted down and killed. Moving to Florida had seemed like a good solution while he was in Arizona, but it turned out to be the worst situation he ever experienced.

I hadn't talked with my son much while he lived in Florida. But when everything collapsed, he started calling me daily for about two weeks and telling me about this disaster he was experiencing. He repeatedly said how much he hated me and how I had screwed up his life. He was yelling and cussing.

I let him know that what he said made sense to me. I also had thought that my parents had wrecked my life. As we continued talking, he became more positive. He knew I had experienced a similar situation, though not at such a drastic levels.

The more we talked on the phone, the more our conversations turned to the good. His revelations were not having a negative influence on me. In fact, they made me realize how deeply I loved him and how I was wide open to helping him in a way that would be life-changing for both of us.

After multiple conversations, Ian decided to come to Colorado and live with me. But before that could happen, I had to help him find "solutions" to his problems in Florida. When he finally did arrive at my house, life was available to him in a different way.

Our conversations were encouraging to me because I had learned to keep my mind and heart focused on God's love and promises, and what God had changed in my life. I wasn't stuck on the fears, rage, and financial problems that made Ian's life a disaster.

When Ian came to my home, he saw a small townhouse with only one available bedroom. But it was mine, and to me it was my new life's kingdom. My home was warm, comfortable, and orderly. I'd had it cleaned, painted, and outfitted with new carpets, tile floors, and nice window covers. I enjoyed living there. There was new furniture, and some really nice things made it look manly but classy. I had a nice office area and a lounging room filled with family photos and all kinds of memorabilia from the times I had spent enjoying the outdoors, friends, and all things I loved doing. Outdoors the place was surrounded by mountains, which could be seen through the windows. My friends used to come to my house just to hang out in the lounge.

I let Ian have my master bedroom. I slept in my camper, parked in the outdoor parking lot. But after three months, the town home association wouldn't let me sleep there, so I moved back inside in my lounge. I used a floor mat for sleeping and each morning when I woke, I turned the room back into a lounge. I loved that my son was safe in my master bedroom, and the whole house was his to use and enjoy. What I wanted most was to stop controlling his symptoms and let God's love be revealed through me to him. Fixing a child is a non-event compared to loving one.

Pain Provides Either Change or a Chain

What we remember or forget depends on whether we keep changing or become chained to a negative path. Many things I did in the past were wrong, including trying to control everyone and everything. My heart was broken about some of those things. But now, as I realized I was not able to fix myself or anyone else, I let go of trying to control everyone.

I had paid the price for my mistakes in brokenness and heartbreak. But the Lord loved me, forgave me, and gave me life-changing insights. When I experienced negatives but stayed connected with God in faith, my hardships became a healthy and adventurous journey. The bad turned to good. The outcomes were so positive, I no longer avoided confronting life's problems. They helped me experience the kingdom of God on earth. Going through hardships, instead of getting run over by them or running away from them, gave me freedom, peace, and joy—which contradicts what I used to think hardships brought! As the book of Acts says, "We must go through many hardships to enter the kingdom of God" (14:22).

What I Could Control

Still, there were some things I could control that helped turn negative situations into positive outcomes. When I handled my thoughts and habits wisely, the opportunity for change became clear. I was able to spend time with others discussing events I experienced and how I processed them. I listened to them reflect on what I said, which gave me a different perspective. I developed the habit of writing and talking about the good that came out of bad situations, and remembering and replaying positive thoughts. Focusing on my gratefulness to God provided very good feelings.

I enjoy watching TV, listening to radio, and reading entertaining books, but I took up a new priority: learning about God, considering my life, and connecting the dots between problems and solutions. No longer would I allow entertainment to control my time. I kept my mind available all day and every day to hear from God.

I realized that if I wanted to change, my thoughts and habits were the only things over which I had control. (I don't mean I can change everything that I want to change about myself. That is very clear to me now. But I can change some things.) I can't control others or life's circumstances, but I do have some control over myself and the things I think about and decide. The good news about developing a new set of habits was that I now focused on my own concerns and not others' shortcomings. I really did not care if anyone else got on board with the way I perceived life or my expectations, because I was discovering many positive things about myself.

After getting to the roots of some of my problems, there came a time when I realized some things I had done had affected my mother negatively. It all came together mentally, emotionally, and spiritually. So I wrote her on Christmas day. The next chapter was the letter I sent. I hoped it would help break the "White family chain" of our lives being stuck on the wrong path.

Breaking the Chain That Prevented Change

Another Letter Sent to Mom on Christmas

Good morning, Mom.

Merry Christmas!
I trust this will lift your spirit and encourage you. Get out the Kleenex!

I have had this in mind to write for about six months, but today seems like a great day to finally write. Obviously I have had much time and many things to reflect on over the last three years. Regardless of the negative situation of my divorce and its fallout, I can honestly say I am a blessed man and *free*. I wish I had done many things differently, as we all do, but I am grateful for the grace God has given me; and others have provided me a huge measure of grace as well. Being the father of two children I now understand how much parents need to give grace, and how desperately their children require it—whether they think they need it or not.

You have given an extraordinary amount of grace to me. Knowing you, about right now you are minimizing your achievement. *Don't!*

As I have reflected over the last years and looked at my behavior and how it contributed to my problems, it has been painful to the core. I have wept more tears in the last three years than the previous forty. I am grateful for the tears; I suspect they will allow for change.

I have gone back mentally into my youth, looking at the roots of my life's decisions. I wanted to understand why I made them, how I made them, and what I could have done differently had Christ been with me. Obviously, at the age of fourteen, we can barely get ourselves out of a wet paper bag. But it gave me insight on how God would have wanted it to go, how he planned it originally to be, and the options I had available to me if I had been spiritually attuned. I can hear you saying, "But Steve, you didn't know Christ." That is true, but seeing now that there were ways God would have led me allows me to see what and how he does things and how wise he is. It allows me to understand my own hurts and how I hurt others by protecting myself. And I see how differently God would have it. It's refreshing to see that I don't have to operate the way I did, and that God's wisdom really works.

I have been forgiven by you and by God, and I am free in that forgiveness. It is also why I am free to write this. I want to let you know some of the things I have seen, and free you from things that have haunted you regarding me at one time or another in your life. We were both in survival mode, suffering things we didn't want to experience and that were not part of our plans for life. I am beginning to understand better what you must have gone through when your life fell apart. Based on my own experience in the last few years, I can only imagine what you were going through. Nightmare on Elm Street sounds like a fair description of what you must have experienced when you and Dad blew apart.

Beyond that, you had to deal with the hurt and anger that I caused. Wow, what a mess. I know these things are all normal in the real world, but I want you to understand some things that are important for me to say about that situation.

Even though it is true that I did not have God in my life back then, the fact is that I sinned against you. There is no way to minimize it. In your mind I can just hear you saying, "No. I sinned against you, Steve." Was I right? Well, that is another story.

My sin was real and it had an effect on both of us. I was rebellious, angry, hateful, and revengeful—and I directed that anger at everyone. At my age I knew what I was doing. I didn't know the consequences, but I didn't care. I was serving myself. I had the option to be grateful for you, and you were trying your best. I could have tried to understand and be supportive in even the smallest way. But I didn't. I had only myself in mind. I did mean and sneaky things and I did them to hurt and punish you. I was in total rebellion. I was critical, judgmental, and distant for many years. I totally dishonored your position as my mother. I know now that regardless of the mess, God does not allow me to dishonor my parents. Period. End of story. There is no provision for dishonoring parents for anyone! I did, and it was a grievous sin for which I am now ashamed. What I did was dark, ugly, and just plain wrong. Thank God it did not happen in ancient Israel; they would have stoned me at the gates of the city, and I would still be piled under the heap! What a picture.

I was wrong for the way I treated you, ignored you, and dishonored your position as a parent. What a fool I was. Admit it. It's OK. I know you sinned and blew it, too. The truth is you were doing your best, trying to provide comfort, shelter, food, and care. I rejected that and rebelled against it. My arrogance has gotten me into a lot of trouble. It also gave me the idea that I could do a better job as a parent and husband. I made a "life rule" that I would never let happen to my family what happened to me. You have to admit that is pretty arrogant, regardless of how understandable it is.

They say the proof is in the pudding. I stayed arrogant. Regardless of my good intentions to change, I had no skills, tools, knowledge, or wisdom to pull it off. I only had a commitment to my intentions with an intensity powered from hell. I was a loose cannon with an attitude. I was deceived in thinking I had a chance to accomplish being a better parent and husband.

I know God has forgiven me. And I know you have, too, and you did it a long time ago. So I am not asking you for forgiveness, for I already have that from you. I am asking you to consider what I have done in hurting you, and what you have done in hurting me. Free yourself of any lingering threads of guilt of what you did. You were no less of a great mom than I was a great son. We both blew it. Our sins are black and ugly, and both of us have paid more for them than our accounts could provide in repayment. We have suffered. God grieved for us and would have walked us both down a better path, but neither of us chose it. We chose our own path when dealing with divorce and raising our children.

You know I have always wanted to break the chain of our family sins. I made a vow many years ago to break the chain. I assumed it would be by never suffering through a divorce. Well, I screwed that up for good.

I am somewhat less arrogant today than in the past. I have no idea how to break the chain of sin, but I believe it is still possible. The chain may be linked to the heart. I have had my heart broken, as you have. Maybe two broken hearts is the start of a new link of spiritual freedom and blessing instead of a chain of sin. Maybe the chain can become a spiritual conduit rather than a chain of victimization, abuse, arrogance, rebellion, bitterness, or anger. I have repented of the sins of a rebellious son. Mom, I am so sorry for my sin against you. I mean it sincerely. I am truly sorry for how wrongly I treated you in the past. I have wept over my sins and do so now as I write.

I pray for God's blessing on your life in disproportion to how poorly I treated you. I trust the Lord will bless you extraordinarily beyond the treatment you received for many years. I do know what this means to you. I have two rebellious children myself, and I know I have a portion of responsibility for creating any situation that brought evil into their lives. They are suffering in part due to my sins, and in part due to yours and Dad's. I have forgiven you and Dad. I know you have forgiven me. God has forgiven us.

I can only hope and have faith that God will somehow use this new link to bring about change. It may be that you and I are the first to truly repent for the sins of our family—and our own sins of parenting and ignoring God's ways. What I lacked all along was a heart that allowed for change. Maybe now I have one. I hope this is part of the divine plan. I am asking God to break the bonds of the White family sins. I don't know them all, but I will be faithful to confess the ones God shows me. I pray that somehow God will restore the children in our family to their parents, their heavenly Father, and down through the years with their children. Who knows? Maybe you will get the chance to be a great-grandmother.

I sure am honored that you are my mother. I was delighted beyond words to have you come to Florida to see my personality training session and what God is producing in your son—and for others to see my mom. Thanks for who you are and what you put up with for so long.

Now you can argue and debate the points all you want. Go get more tissues.

Love, Steve.

Being open and honest and taking responsibility, choosing humility and connecting to my mom, and telling others about my issues—this brings it all out of the darkness and into the light.

SECTION 5

PROOF IS IN
THE PUDDING!

PROOF IN
THE PUDDING

The proof is in the pudding, or so they say. And for me and my life, there needed to be some proof of real change. I couldn't fake having peace and joy when the worst type of events hit the fan in a relatively short period. The list of events you will read in the next few pages starts at the beginning of my marriage. I do it this way so you can see my whole lifestyle that went on for decades. But the worst came about fourteen years into our marriage.

I have already told some stories that showed changes in me and my life perspectives. It took a few years, but I had become open to discovering my part of our marriage problems. When I learned to focus my time, energy, and thoughts on my own issues—and what needed changing within me—I wasn't under pressure to fix others, and I did not want fake changes. I had learned that when bad events happen, they come with a promise from God that "in all things God works for the good of those who love him, who have been called according to his purpose" (Romans 8:28).

Half the time into the marriage, the events going on around me were so negative, they motivated me to stay connected to God. I was the cause of some of them, while others had nothing to do with me. Some of the events sent me down a wrong path early in the marriage, and some led me to discover my problems, gain insights, and experience positive changes. And some of the events show beyond any question that God and his love are real.

The following events are listed in sequence. Once I got married, my best intentions started going south. In fact, it started the day after our marriage:

- My wife became ill the day after our wedding, and she stayed ill for twelve years.
- We started fighting the day after our marriage, and we continued fighting for nineteen years. We fought almost daily, at best weekly.
- Debbie had a miscarriage within months of getting married, and then we had a son the first year.
- We moved to Grand Junction in western Colorado just after the first year. We arrived near "Black Sunday," the day Exxon Oil pulled out of the region and the local economy collapsed. The economic collapse was written about in national newspapers.
- When I got hired in Colorado, I made a promise and signed an agreement to stay with the company as a salesman for a minimum of one year. Work was objectionable because of the consequences of Black Sunday, as well as other problems.
- I worked three jobs for the first three years so I could pay our doctor bills and afford pain medication for my wife. After that, I maintained two jobs for most of the next ten years.
- My wife had another miscarriage, and then we had a daughter after the third year.
- I hated my primary job. My boss was an alcoholic who hated salespeople. I had not been hired by him, nor did I know about him when I took the job. You will find out more about him in the story "Good Morning America."

- My job sucked, I sucked, and everything sucked. But I couldn't quit because no company would insure my wife due to her illnesses.
- After realizing I was stuck at the job, I made a decision to be the best I could be at my job.
- In the third year of our marriage, I met a guy in a large gymnasium. He and I were the only ones there. He told me I ought to go to the church at Redstone, Colorado. I thought of telling him where to go. I lived two hours away. I thought he was crazy. Immediately after telling me this, he left the gym.
- Two years later we moved to Glenwood Springs, Colorado, and I remembered what the man in the gymnasium said. Go figure!
- In that fifth year of our marriage, I met the pastor at that church in Redstone. His name was Doug Self.
- We started marital counseling with Doug Self.
- Between the fifth and sixth years, my wife was hospitalized sixteen times in twelve months. We assumed she was going to die.
- Then we moved to the Crystal River, just a few miles from Redstone and near that church.

I started seeing things about myself. I realized that if I didn't experience God in a very real way, my family could see that I could not possibly help them turn their own lives to the good. I began focusing on my issues.

- For years I was paying seventeen doctors some small amount monthly because of all the medical expenses from my wife's illnesses.
- About twelve years into the marriage, my wife was healed of her diseases. Our elders prayed for her on a Friday. Saturday she was healed. The healing was a miracle. Monday we went to her doctor; even her doctor said it was a miracle. She also got a disability settlement. We paid off the doctors.

- At fourteen, my son started doing drugs. He told me he got some of his drugs from a counselor who worked at a drug rehab center in our area.

From this point on, God had begun a change in me and prepared me for upcoming events. The friends I had in Colorado would agree that I was experiencing changes and peace. I lived the verse that says, "Do not be anxious about anything, but in everything, by prayer and petition, with thanksgiving, present your requests to God. And the peace of God, which transcends all understanding, will guard your hearts and your minds in Christ Jesus" (Phil. 4:6–7).

- For two years we spent a lot of time and money on my son's drug situation. I considered if my actions had pushed him into drugs.
- At sixteen, Ian got arrested for drugs, and we sent him to a rehab center.
- Within three weeks of the first rehab, he was back into drugs worse than ever. The situation was destroying my family.
- After the rehab, my son ran away four times. The first time was the day I was running a marathon. I cried a lot during the run.
- The third time was with an eighteen-year-old who was connected with the Polish Mafia in Chicago. Together they planned to run drugs for them. Ian came back home because their plans fell apart.
- He ran away again for a fourth time on New Year's Day. He said we would never see him again. He was sixteen.
- While on my knees wailing after my son walked out the door, I heard the soft voice of God say, "Put your baby in the basket." I knew that referred to Moses' sister, Miriam, putting the infant Moses in a basket and letting him float down the Nile River to prevent Pharaoh from killing him. Pharaoh's daughter pulled him out of the river and raised him as her son (Exod. 2:3–10).

- On a Sunday in January we told a small group of people at our church the basics of the situation. They prayed for us and asked God for a miracle so we could find our son.
- The next morning we found out he was headed to Mexico to run drugs for the Mexican Mafia. He would be leaving Tuesday afternoon. At the time we didn't know where he was.
- That afternoon, a couple in our community committed to pay all expenses for a rehabilitation program called New Horizons, which is based in Indiana and the Dominican Republic. It would cost $50,000 a year, and if he was in the Dominican Republic program, it could keep him until he was twenty-one. That would cost $250,000! None of us knew where Ian was.
- In a miraculous way on Tuesday, the police found our son a few hours before he was to leave for Mexico. A guy named Tudie at my church said he had been told by God on Monday to go to Burger King and ask a manager where Ian lived and then go find him and take him to dinner. Tudie had no idea what was going on, but knew God had spoken to him; so he did it. Tuesday I had called him to let him know my son was heading to Mexico, but that no one knew where he was. Tudie told me. I called our police captain, who called the captain in the town where Ian was. That captain found Ian in someone's apartment an hour before he was leaving for Mexico.
- Tuesday night I had to sign my son over to the rehab program, relieving me of all parental control. It was an uncomfortable decision.
- In six months we went to Indiana to see him, as they were about to send him to the Dominican Republic.
- Six months later we flew to the Dominican Republic. As we were going to the rehab facility in Jarabacoa, a van of men ran our taxi van off the road and surrounded the vehicle. They started pounding on it. I assumed they meant to rape my wife and daughter, so I planned a way to kill a few of them and get killed if I had to in order to save my wife and daughter. We discussed it while they surrounded our taxi. Then the men went away. My wife was hysterical. And I don't mean funny!

- A day later we found out the van had a sign in Spanish on the back saying *Se Vende*. That meant it was for sale. I never knew that. While heading back from the rehab facility, we got pulled off the road three more times.
- Two days after we returned home, I was in the middle of doing a seminar at a hotel when I got an emergency call. My wife's brother had stabbed his wife to death in front of one of his children.
- I took two weeks off work and drove to the prison in northern California with my wife and her parents.
- During this trip, I was connected with God and had such peace that I was able to make a difference in her parents' lives. I felt God's presence the whole time.
- At the prison, my wife's father touched the one-inch glass between his hand and his son's. He would never touch his son again. I told God I would die if that ever happened to me.
- We had to go to the house where the murder took place. The police warned me it would be shocking. His parents waited in the car while I walked in.
- The living room had blood all over the floor, dog crap was everywhere, and trash and motorcycle parts were all over the living room. The bathtubs were also filled with dog crap. There was no way to manage or minimize the shock for his parents.
- We spent the next year and a half walking through that disaster and exploring the possibility of adopting Debbie's brother's two children.
- The discovery of what lead to the murder was a big story in the California newspapers. Her brother's family was the first part of a new California state plan about preventing murder and life disasters in marriages. Meanwhile my son was in the Dominican Republic going through his rehab program and living a pretty miserable life.
- During this time my mother called and said my stepfather was dying. He died within a few months.
- About this time I was named the National Sales Trainer for the corporation I worked for. I had decided I would be the best I could be, and it paid off.

- Our son got out of the New Horizons program eighteen months after entering. He was rehabilitated, and in our minds the changes he experienced were very positive.

- Ian moved back to Colorado and went into a reentry program near our home.

- Our friends Mick and Jan Bennett started a reentry program with our son as their first client. They did it for free. He stayed there three months. Then he decided to move back home, reestablish a new life, and repair the old wounds of our family. We were delighted!

- About three months after my son moved back home, my wife went to her high school reunion. When she returned, she said she was leaving us. She filed for divorce.

- I received the divorce papers on Mother's Day. My wife drained our bank account and withdrew all the money the bank allowed as a loan. She then moved to Arizona.

- She did not even say good-bye to our son. She took my daughter with her and moved in with her high school sweetheart, whom she had met at the reunion. I assumed I was now at the pinnacle of pain, but my pain was only beginning.

- Because of this event, my son went over the edge. He started doing drugs again, and he even started dealing them. His new perspective could be summed up this way: "Screw life." He continued to live with me during the divorce proceedings and his drug dealings.

- My stepmother called and said my dad was dying. He died during the divorce.

- During the divorce my son had a drug deal go very bad, and someone was about to shoot his friend who was part of the deal. My son shot the guy point-blank with my shotgun. He came home and told me he thought the guy was dead.

- I told my son he had to turn himself in. He agreed, so I took him to the sheriff's department. I expected the charge would be murder. This made the divorce a non-event. I had no idea sorrow and heartache could be experienced at this level. Yet I had an unexplainable peace I could not deny. I still loved God and my life deeply, and I spent much time sitting in my heavenly Father's lap. This was unlike anything I had ever experienced.

- During the divorce, the criminal proceedings for my son continued, and I went to my dad's funeral. That was also a personal disaster.
- In one week I went to the divorce hearing on a Monday, to the arraignment for my son on Tuesday, and had a root canal on Wednesday. It is a no-brainer which day was the highlight of my week.
- The divorce took seventeen months. From beginning to end, it was a disaster.
- Three months after the divorce was final, my ex informed me she was getting married. And it was *not* to the guy she had moved in with.
- After the divorce, my daughter sent me a letter saying she did not want to talk to me or ever see me again. She even told me not to write her. I had no idea why.
- For years I sent her cards and letters with checks for gifts on holidays and birthdays, but I sent them to my address because she mandated that I not stay in touch. I kept them in a box for years. I was sad for her when I wrote, but had peace and joy about my life. Years later, my daughter reconnected with me; she got all the gifts I had saved. The postmarks on the envelopes proved she was loved the whole time she had avoided me.
- My son was in jail. My daughter was gone and not talking to me. My dad was dead, and so was my stepdad. And my wife was gone. I was in financial ruin. And yet I experienced a peace and a level of joy that I could not understand—or fake.
- A few years later I heard from my mother that my daughter had gotten married, and I had a grandson.

I had no guarantee I could reconnect with my daughter or that anything would change. But I did have a guarantee that God would still turn it all to the good. I just didn't know how it would happen. Giving my daughter away at her wedding had been one of my life's dreams.

And now it was lost. Yet during all of this, I still had peace in my heart and mind, and my love for my daughter grew stronger.

God can and does turn bad things to the good for those who love him. It might take time, and it might not happen at all the way we think it should, but God will make bad things turn to the good. Faith in God is what we need, for that is what brings about the experience of change. This is a promise from the Bible, and I never want to forget it.

Too many things happened in a short period of time for me to begin to pretend I got through it on my own. The proof is in the pudding. God had accomplished many changes within me, and he was revealing a new set of attitudes that comforted me and influenced others.

Ian graduated from New Horizon in Indiana and their
Dominican Republic program

THREE LIFE EVENTS

These next three events that happened to me do not directly relate to being blinded by good intentions, but they show what God can do in a person's life. I want to write about the voice of God, the hand of God, and how God turns all things to the good of those who love him.

The Voice of God

Our son had run away and was headed to Mexico. He told us we would never see him again! The day after he left to run drugs for the Mexican Mafia, my wife was filling out paperwork for a rehab program we had heard about. She had requested the application forms a week before, so we could look at the program. It quickly became clear that we could not afford it. We had no money and no possibility of getting a loan or of selling all we had to pay for it.

The program we were considering required three months of preparation and many interviews with the program's managers for participants to get in. Even if we could have afforded it, we had no idea where our son was.

Deb was sitting on the couch frantically filling out the papers. As I watched her, I became irritated because I knew it was a waste of time and energy. I came up behind her and said, "This is a ridiculous waste of time."

Right there I heard the voice of God say, "This isn't of her. Leave her alone."

I stopped mid-sentence and told Deb to "do whatever you feel you need to do." I walked off, assuming God was just giving her time to feel better, and that filling out the paperwork would make her feel like she had tried to do something to fix things. I thought it was a waste of time, but I knew I had heard from God to back off.

The next day a couple agreed to fund Ian's entire rehab program. It would cost anywhere from $90,000 to $250,000. It had taken my wife more than eight hours to complete the paperwork, and it turned out that paperwork was the key to getting our son accepted in the program—in spite of our not having the money to pay for it on our own.

Had I stopped her, we would not have been able to get him into the program in time, and he would have been in Mexico running drugs. The program accepted him on Tuesday, and the police found him the same day, just hours before he got on a bus to Mexico. That story is another book in itself!

I had gotten more familiar with hearing a soft voice that would come to me unexpectedly. When it happened, I realized God was talking to me. The voice brought insights that were smarter than I could possibly be. To me, this proves beyond doubt that God talks to us. It takes time to learn to listen and recognize and obey God's voice, but once you have heard that voice, it is a life-changing experience.

The Hand of God

The day of the shooting when I turned my son in to the police, as we were on the way to the police station, I told my son he needed to tell them the entire truth and not leave out any details. He agreed. I called the police as we were heading there and told them to send an ambulance to the place of the shooting. We passed the ambulance on the way to the police station. When we arrived, my son told the police everything truthfully, and eventually their investigation proved all that he said was true. Telling the truth had a very positive influence.

Based on his involvement with drugs, guns, and shootings, some policemen estimated my son's prison sentence would at the very least be twenty-five years. I get sick just thinking about that. As I sat alone with a policeman and told him what I knew, the police department compared it to what my son was telling them. They were making sure there were no contradictions. The sentencing would obviously ruin Ian's life. I assumed I would die before he got out of prison. In my mind, I was at the prison like my ex-wife's father, putting my hand on the inch-thick glass window on one side, with my son doing the same on the other. We would never touch each other again. I pictured that in my mind, and I wondered if that was going to be true of us.

My son's life was a disaster. Yet while all of this was happening, with me in the middle of it, I was in a very odd state of mind. My heart was broken, but I was not crying. I was calm. My friends Doug Self and Charlie Hill were at the station with me. I felt like I was sitting on God's lap with his arm around me. It was God's intervention in my life that provided peace. Even while my heart was broken for my son, I felt a comfort within me. There was no temptation to focus on and replay the negatives. I remember I was heartbroken, and all the information I was hearing was negative, yet within myself I was at peace. I remember thinking that feeling this way was not normal. I felt like something unexpected was going to happen, something that made no sense logically.

About four hours after the shooting, Terry Wilson, the chief of police, came up to me and said, "There must be a God looking out for your kid. I just talked to the guy your son shot. He was walking around the hospital! (I almost fell out of my chair.) He was hit in the heart area by the wadding from the shotgun shell. The wad burned a hole through the fleece jacket and burned his skin, but there were no visible pellet marks. The pellets were stuck in the fleece jacket. I think the hand of God saved that guy."

This was a jaw-dropping event for me, and I mean my jaw literally dropped. The way a shotgun shell works is that the wadding holds the pellets. It is physically impossible for the pellets to be behind the wad, because the wad is what pushes the pellets out of the barrel. The pellets have to come out first, and then the wadding. The man who was shot was less than five feet away from the shotgun's barrel. The pellets hit the gun the man was holding and damaged his hand extensively (apparently his hand was at his heart level). I have no trouble believing that God saved the man's life by using an angel. As I looked at all the details of the event, it became clear that God was not just a feeling, but a Presence in this whole situation.

God Turns All Things to the Good

I do not understand how things unfolded during my son's court experiences. It did not happen the way anyone expected. Some others involved in the drug deal and shooting were sent to state prison. My son spent ninety days in the county jail, and then was put on probation.

I had two noteworthy experiences involving friends who knew about the shooting. Five years after the event they each had different people tell them a story about a shooting that had occurred in the area where we lived. (The event they were describing was the story about my son and me and the shooting.) The people who talked to my friends did not know they knew me and my son, and my friends did not reveal that.

Both people mentioned the shooting and what happened afterward. They told my friends that the relationship they heard about between a son who had shot someone and his father was very encouraging, based on the father helping his son be honest and open in telling the police everything he had done. They said the son's candor caused things to work out to the best outcome. The police confirmed everything the son said, so they knew he was telling the truth.

My friends heard these accounts two weeks apart. Neither knew that the other had heard the same story from someone else. Each person described the basics of what happened, and how the legal issues could have turned out if the son had handled things differently. They knew how the legal process works. They both told my friends that having heard what took place with my son caused them to realize that things could have destroyed our relationship and both of our lives.

They said the father's influence on the son made a huge impact on the outcome!

When my friends told me the story, I went home and wept. It took me weeks to stop crying whenever I thought about it. I remember traveling often by plane, thinking about what the people told my friends, and getting so teary, I would hide my eyes from those sitting next to me. To me, this event is proof of just how deeply God loves us and how he turns all things to the good.

More Proof of God Turning the Bad to the Good

This story started thirty years ago. I knew God, and I knew I was a Christian. But I had not been following him the way he wants us to so we can experience a positive change in our lives. In fact, at that time I was experiencing mostly negative changes. I was at a place of brokenness that finally helped me realize I needed to connect deeper to God—and stay committed to following him as a disciple for the rest of my life. I decided to make a change that I did have control over, and it was a good decision. The decision was about my job. I wish I had made this type of decision toward my wife, my family, and the rest of life much earlier, because God used my job to bring about changes in a very helpful way.

My First Colorado Job

I have already written about my first job when we moved to Colorado being a disaster. I said the outcome was another story—and here it is.

When we arrived in Grand Junction, the Exxon Oil Company had just bailed out of the region. No one knew it was going to happen, and it caused an economic disaster throughout Western Colorado. The owners of the franchise company I worked for had bought the business during a great economy. They bought the business at a very cheap price because the previous owner had lost the franchise after doing some really bad things. This happened just months before I moved there.

I had met only one of the owners, and I had not met the new office manager. The owners operated the same type of business my uncle and cousin had worked at for many years. Their original business was in the Roaring Fork Valley, east of Grand Junction and between Aspen and Vail. That business was very successful. The new office manager they hired for Grand Junction was someone who had worked for the same world corporation I now work for. The corporation provides franchise-owned businesses and corporate-owned businesses all over the world. The owners did not know this new office manager very well, but because he had worked for the larger corporation, it seemed he would be a great hire.

Before I started the job I was sent to a sales training session in California. My uncle and cousin warned me that when I went to the training session, I would be very uncomfortable about how they trained us to be salespeople. But my uncle said not to worry, because we would not have to sell the way they teach. He said they only wanted the sales team to know the data about their systems, and did not really expect them to be the kind of salesperson the training suggested.

Before taking this new job in Grand Junction, I had been very successful in real estate sales. That was why my relatives recommended that the owners hire me. I planned to get back into real estate after working for this business for one year. I would use this new job to get known in a new community, and I would be paid a salary rather than depending on the straight commission for my real estate sales. This would help me stay on the right financial track for that first year.

My uncle was right about the type of instruction I received at the sales training session. It quickly became clear that I did not want to be like the typical salespeople that I had also experienced in Real Estate. In the 1980s most people hated a Realtor's sales people. As I had started selling in Real Estate I knew that I would have to be non-typical to be a great sales person, and that was my desire and why my Real Estate sales were successful and so influential with home buyers.

The First Week

When I got to Grand Junction, the first week's events presented a serious set of five problems. First, I found out how bad the previous owner's reputation was. He and his salesman were not at all well liked. This put me into a panic. The second problem was the collapse of the local economy. The third problem came when my wife and I moved. She hated it and experienced a mental breakdown. Fourth, the new manager let me know that he hated salespeople and assumed I was a complete moron.

Fifth, my uncle showed me a letter the sales trainer sent him about me. My uncle thought it was funny, but I had no idea what caused that trainer to say what he did, or what that letter would prove at some point in the future. Here is part of what the sales trainer said:

> Be aware of this guy Steve, because he is going to try and change the whole system. He was obviously a great salesperson in real estate before you hired him, but I think he may cause a major problem in your company because I think he will try to change all of us in the corporation!

The Second Week

The second week came with another set of problems. My wife was getting much sicker, and she wanted to move back to California. I found out that people in Grand Junction all hated salespeople because the city had been overtaken by many companies that had typical, pushy salesmen. Because the local economy had been booming, sales companies from all over the country had moved there or started more businesses.

I discovered that because of all the problems my company had caused, no one had even called them in the previous three months. I also found out that there were so many competitors in sales, the whole town was fed up with being solicited. Some of my competitors had large groups doing phone soliciting. One had fifty people on the phone, and another, thirty-five. Many other companies also had large sales forces. There were so many phone soliciting groups, the town was being re-solicited every two and a half days. At that time the town's population was about 150,000. Many were experiencing twelve to eighteen solicitations each day! I heard from some customers that they were calling the police department to get salespeople out of their homes!

My worst fear was realizing that to survive, I had to start soliciting to help support the company I worked for. And I hated soliciting.

Good Morning America

During the first three months of my new job, I had never experienced so many bad things within a community or a business. I could not figure out how I was going to make anything work out for the company. My wife and I fought on a daily basis, and her illness became a major problem.

While all this was going on, the manager and I were finding it extremely difficult to relate. He threatened to kill me, and I knew it was not a joke. I realized he had some very serious mental problems. It became so bad, I had to work from my home until the owners either fired him or sent him for psychiatric treatment. This guy wound up killing himself!

I was staying at home one morning, trying to avoid that manager. I was so wiped out, all I was doing was sitting and watching TV. I was furious, disgusted, panicked, and more emotionally drained than I had ever experienced.

The program *Good Morning America* came on. Joan Lunden, the sweet news lady who was one of the best-loved women in America, was about to introduce a comedian who was famous for making funny comments about good things turning bad. He told her he had a good morning getting ready to come to her program, but then something bad happened when his daughter called and said, "Dad, I am getting married now! I am marrying the Culligan Man."

Everyone on the show was laughing. Culligan was known for having sales people, and the comedian made it clear that a sales person was marrying his daughter. I didn't see anything funny about this. I was working for Culligan, it was not working out in a good way, and I didn't like the concept of typical sales people. I got so mad, I took off a shoe and threw it at the TV. Then I jumped off the couch and stormed out of my house, screaming and cussing. I was stomping around outside yelling at nothing in particular, my mind about to explode.

A Good Decision

I could not control the previous reputation of the company in Grand Junction, the city's business climate, and all the lousy things going on between me and my manager, my wife, and my life in general. I hated being a salesperson in this stinking situation. I also knew I couldn't quit the job because I had signed a contract and promised my uncle and cousin that I would stay for at least a year. Also, the company's insurance carrier was covering my wife, and it was costing them tens of thousands of dollars. I knew no other insurance company would take her and pay for her pre-existing health problems. So while I was standing outside, I realized I had to do something different.

I stood out there and pondered what I could control. I knew if I didn't change my thoughts, attitudes, and commitments, I would stay on a very negative life path. I knew that quitting the job was wrong, and even if I did quit, I knew that the real estate business in this city had also become a disaster.

The decision for me became very clear. I would become the best sales person I possibly could. I would learn to do whatever it took to make things work out not only at my level, but also at a level I never experienced. I committed to making changes in sales people's typical sales tactics, and I wanted to change the typical corporate concepts of selling. I would learn how to get out of the box and learn what works and what doesn't. If I stayed on the path I had been on, my life would be miserable, and I was not going to put up with that anymore. So that day I made an out-loud commitment to learn to be the best salesperson I could be.

Honoring and Serving Others

Things started to change. I learned how to prioritize the customer's needs and concerns and to connect to customers at a new level. I started thinking from the customer's perspective. I focused on honoring and serving them. I became open to new kinds of thinking on what to do and how to do things that would create interest, curiosity, and desire. Before long, people wanted to meet with me and do business with our company. Because I could not cross the fence and find greener grass with a new job, I had to learn how to make the grass greener on my side of the fence. I wanted it to become the best grass possible.

Of course I was not doing everything perfectly. Nothing has ever been perfect for any day of my entire career. But the changes in my style as a salesperson were real, and they had a positive influence on customers. I started making a lot of sales, and people said they loved doing business with me. I got all kinds of referrals for the rest of my sales career. Things were working out at a level I had never experienced, and it stayed on that track for nineteen years with the franchise company.

About nine years into my job, I decided I wanted to help others break away from the typical way of doing things. I wanted to help them see things from a customer's point of view. So I started doing free training for three days at three times during the year, and I created a group called Western Regional Culligan Sales Association. I did it for free because I enjoyed helping others learn the things I had learned, and I wanted to help those in our company rise to new levels of salesmanship. Our group stayed connected for ten years, and all enjoyed improved sales.

This was the day at a National Convention in Arizona when
I was a sales person who had won a top award as one of the best
sales people in the Nation. The two men were the CEO
and COO of Culligan International

A Brand New Job

In my nineteenth year with the franchise, I was asked to be a
regional sales trainer for the corporation. The person responsible
for getting me this new job was a corporate sales director who had
been coming to my Western Regional Sales Association for years. Six
months after taking the job, I was asked to become the national sales
trainer. With this new job I would be traveling and helping people
all over the nation.

In my second year as national sales trainer, I was speaking at a
national convention for all the Culligan international companies in
America. I was telling a story about how we need to decide what we
have control over and how to let go of staying stuck on our problems.
The story was about what I experienced when I started with the
Culligan franchise and how it wiped me out. I then told them the
story about the comedian I saw on *Good Morning America.* I had

never told this story in public, and I had not planned on telling it then. It just came out. I got to the part where I was standing outside my house yelling—and then decided to be the best I could be and to influence people in the best way possible to bring about real changes.

I told them that is what I stayed committed to for life. Then it struck me that I had just connected the dots of my new job! What came out was said very softly, and it was a new thought to me as I said it: "I am the National Sales Trainer!" I had never realized that my decision to be the best I could be as a salesperson and to make real changes in this company was what gave me the new job. I started to choke up in front of the whole group. I just stood there until I finally walked off stage. According to my director, I got a standing ovation.

I have never done anything perfectly. But I have been able to initiate real change and connect to the people I wanted to connect to. And I became the best salesperson I could become. I had done it, and now I was helping others to make the same changes. I have now been with Culligan International as the North American National Sales Trainer for eleven years, and I have been with Culligan system for thirty years. It is the best job I have ever had because I decided to stand on that narrow path, control my thoughts, and experience freedom, peace, and joy in my life and work.

SECTION 6

THE BEST OF THE LAST—A NEW LIFE EXPERIENCE FOR ALL

This is my final section of stories. A few have new things I learned and experienced, and some are about what brought me beyond what I ever expected. All reveal concepts I learned to accomplish good changes. I hope they will prove that these concepts work for all of us and will continue to work for us the rest of our lives—if we are open to experiencing and learning. The way God uses them can bring a new life experience for all!

KARI EXPERIENCED THE PROCESS OF THOSE CONCEPTS

Not long ago I spent a week in Arizona with my daughter Kari. She read a draft manuscript of this book and told me what she thought about it and how it helped her. She pulled out her journal and showed me what she had been dealing with for the last year—and where she had come to land in the last few months.

She had seen a continuous pattern in her life and realized the problem was not the people around her, but rather her attitude and expectations about life and others. In her state of mind, it would not have mattered if some circumstances changed; she still would not be at peace. These are some of the things Kari discovered were stealing her peace and taking her down the wrong path over and over again.

She didn't realize it, but what she had written in her journal tied into each concept I have already discussed here. We don't have to be aware of every concept to experience it, but she said it helped to realize she was experiencing them. She wants to remember the process and the concepts, so she had me read her journal and connect it to all the ideas in this book.

Kari said she had been asking God to expose her problems regarding her marriage and parental struggles. I told her it would be encouraging for others to read about her experiences, and she gave me permission to use her journal entries. Try thinking from her perspective as you read this. I numbered and listed the concepts she had learned from me at the top of some of her paragraphs. I also put in the verses that prove why she experienced changes. Here is what she wrote:

Kari's Journal Content

I have all these expectations for my family, and when they are not met I go down the crapper. I wanted things to work out for my family the way I thought they should—with Casen doing his homework and Jason helping clean house and working with Casen on his homework.

Cooking healthy meals. Doing the laundry. Having the house picked up. Doing my Bible study. Working out at least four times a week. Those were my smaller expectations. Bigger expectations include going to school, work, and being able to assist my husband with his fireman job. I want to make it possible for him to sleep and rest when he needs to. Another big expectation is for my family to spend more quality time together.

These are all things I felt had to be working in my life for me to feel like I am doing what's right. Or these were the things that needed to happen in order for me to be at peace.

How do I treat others when these expectations are not met? I am pretty bad. I get snippy with Casen when he asks me for help. I have too many things to do, so I rush him when I play with him. I get irritated with him. Then I pray for more things to meet my increased expectations. I mutter and complain. When I don't get to do my Bible study, I panic and think I'm under attack. I try to read all day. Ignore Casen. Get irritated. Then feel guilty about how I treated him. I've got to make more time to spend with him to make up for my failures, but I feel I need more time in the day.

Jason somehow knows to stay out of my way. I am still snippy and complain to him that I can't do it all. I rudely ask for help. I panic about how we will be able to keep this all going when I start school full time. Now I think maybe I shouldn't even be thinking of going back to school. I still treat others poorly and make them feel it is their fault that I am worn out. How can anyone ask me to do any more? And yet when my husband is busy, I wonder why he doesn't ask me to do more for him. I can't do any more, and I can't do enough. Both thoughts are negative. I want to sit and talk about it, but he doesn't show interest. Hmmm. This is all yucky!

How do I treat myself? I have a dogged attitude. I am a little grasshopper trying to conquer the world. Where is God in all this? I don't get it. I am confused. I thought this is what I'm supposed to do. I'm being respectful and taking care of my family and what God has given me. This attitude is negative and it makes me feel more run down. I beat myself up and feel bad for myself that I have all these things to do. (Key: I have chosen to do all these things for me to feel good.) I get mad at myself that I can't make time for these little things, and when I do make time, the little things keep me from accomplishing my bigger goals.

The way I sometimes treat my family (badly) hurts me. I want to meet these family expectations because this is how I view that things should be done to show love. I love them more than anyone or anything else in the world, and I care about them more than any "to do" list. What is wrong with me?

Wait a minute. My life is being run by what I think love should be. Then I am controlling the actions of my family and justifying it by saying I'm protecting us with love. But God is not running my life. I am using my imagination of what I think God is, and living by my imagination. After all, he is love. It doesn't all fit and run together. Hmmm, this is exactly what my dad's book is about—our intentions blinding us from what is really true. And boy does all this keep us busy, blinded, and confused. I am wondering where God is in all this?

And my anger is not working out at all.

Exposure verses (Ephesians 5:13): "But everything exposed by the light becomes visible." The second half of 1 Corinthians 4:5: "He will bring to light what is hidden in darkness and will expose the motives of men's hearts. At that time each will receive his praise from God."

Concept 1: Exposure

I am struggling with time, control issues, expectations, and anger. I talk too much. How I discipline Casen is not consistent—it alternates between being aggressive and being passive.

Concept 2: Insights

I am aware that my personality is part of the problem. Little things take me out of a peaceful frame of mind. I know I won't be happy no matter what happens unless I take care of me and my expectations. But when I do that, I go down the wrong path. I need to give God my expectations and let him take care of me. I am trying to fix Casen and myself because I think we should be perfect in order to meet God's expectations and keep our family together.

Proverbs 2:3–6, 10 prove these points. "And if you call out for insight and cry aloud for understanding, and if you look for it as for silver and search for it as for hidden treasure, then you will understand the fear of the Lord and find the knowledge of God. For the Lord gives wisdom, and from his mouth come knowledge and understanding.... For wisdom will enter your heart, and knowledge will be pleasant to your soul."

Concept 3: Connecting Patterns

When I don't get these things done, I go down the wrong path. I feel guilt, irritation, and anger—at me and at God. I try to stop doing anything until I hear from God what to do, and still I don't hear anything.

A positive pattern is using time to pray, talk out loud to God, ponder, read, and write. When I realize things are not working out, that is when I get most of my insights.

Concept 4: Controlling My Thought Patterns

When things don't get done, I think there is something wrong with me. I think I don't have enough time. I almost brought about a divorce harping on this topic, and I fear I will do it again. I keep replaying my negative thoughts. I am unrealistic and out of balance.

In a positive vein, I try to control my thoughts with prayer, journaling, and rereading Joyce Meyer's *Battlefield of the Mind*. I am more open, more often, to gaining insights instead of doing things the way I always do.

Concept 5: Discovering How I Let Issues Cause Heart Wounds

My heart wounds come from constantly replaying guilt and "thinking down" on myself. Insights are being overtaken by my negative thoughts, flesh, and Satan. Positive things include talking to my husband, Jason, and calling my dad and talking to him about the things that are bothering me. The verses that affect concepts 4 and 5 are ones already in the book: Romans 12:2 and Romans 8:5–6.

Concept 6: Faith in God Will Provide a New Life

God loves us just the way we are. He does not need to fix us, and by grace he heals and adores us. I am asking God to balance us and that we will trust and believe him in the middle of all this. I am praying we stay on the narrow path, and that we, as a family and individually, give our expectations to God and allow him to work within us. We will stand by God's side and let exposure bring great insights of peace, love, and encouragement.

I want my strengths to blossom in God and to rely on him in my weaknesses. I want to see the same thing for other people's strengths and talents—and I want to build my son's strength and talents. I pray my husband and I find favor in each other and that we all experience and receive God's love and give it freely in Jesus' name.

The only person I have control over is me. The only part I have control over is my thoughts and attitude. Controlling my thoughts will provide the freedom from being stuck on the negative thoughts and letting them control my life. Romans 8:28 is another verse to prove the outcomes: "We know that in all things God works for the good of those who love him ..."

Kari and I talked more about all that I read, and it is exciting for both of us as she realizes how much she is learning about herself and the changes she has experienced. I am thankful she allowed me to read her journal, and we will continue talking about it and walking through her life together. She has been journaling for about two years, and she repeatedly tells me how helpful it is. She continues to read books from her favorite authors, so they are very much like mentors to her. I hope her candor will encourage you that we are all potentially on a similar path.

Now I Want More Exposure

I still want to be awakened to things I am unaware of, so I keep asking God to expose things about me to teach me. I want more exposure even if it causes guilt, irritation, embarrassment, anger, fear, or worry. My daughter Kari experienced this also, and that experience may be true of all of us as we stand at the doorway to change.

I can become both aggressive and passive about being exposed. Thankfully, my bad feelings helped me remember why I wanted to experience internal changes. I chose to battle against the negative thoughts that opposed my being open to new things. It was a struggle, but it helped me realize sooner what I was doing wrong. Then I became grateful for what I was learning about my problems. Change began within me and was from the inside out, not just affecting outward appearances.

I Don't Have an Angry Cell in My Body!

Over the last year I have had a particular thought that I believed was true and that I repeated to myself and a couple of friends when I had some friction with other people. I'd say, "I don't have an angry cell in my body!" I thought that was true, because I had experienced some impressive changes in my management of anger.

Then I had an altercation with my son because he let a bunch of people stay overnight at my house. The day before this happened, we had a conversation about not having people stay overnight. And yet when I came home from camping early the next morning—the day after our conversation about people not staying overnight—I walked into my house with people sleeping all over the place.

I woke them all and told them to leave. Then I went upstairs to my son and woke him and asked him what was going on. I didn't get an answer, so I asked again. He was irritated and didn't say anything, so I asked him why he was acting like this. No answer. Then I asked him again why he allowed these people to stay overnight. By now he had become visibly annoyed.

He went outside and I followed him, asking more questions. Then he got really angry, and he still would not talk to me. I called my friend Doug and told him what happened. I said that I was stunned that my son was mad at me, because I had not been mad at all! I said, "I don't have an angry cell in my body!"

In a day or two, my son called Doug and asked if we could get together with him to discuss what happened. As I listened to Ian tell the story, it was pretty accurate, except when he said I was mad. I disagreed and repeated the same stupid thing: "I don't have an angry cell in my body!"

And I really did believe that. Later in the morning, after the event, I realized I didn't want to be angry. But that was not true during the event itself. When I thought about the way I handled things, it was obvious I had some level of anger when I told everyone to get out of my house—and then kept asking my son why he had done this. I had some kind of anger in me or I would not have reacted that way. And

I would not have kept demanding that my son answer me the way I wanted to hear it, and when I wanted to hear it.

While the three of us we were talking about this, I still didn't get the insight. Fortunately Doug made it very obvious that I was angry—and that the notion of my not having an angry cell in my body was nonsense. Over the past year he had heard me claim that dozens of times. I finally realized I was being ridiculously stupid! How could I have believed I could not be capable of anger? I was now aware of something within me that God exposed.

Deeper Insights

Though I have experienced positive changes in controlling my anger, my thoughts somehow took me in the wrong direction. I am grateful for the exposure and the additional insights in this area. They have allowed me to focus my thoughts on the anger within me in deeper and more helpful ways. Now I want more exposure in other areas.

My faith in God has given me peace, joy, freedom, and love toward my son. We have not spoken again about this event, and I probably won't get any answers to my questions. But I have confronted my ignorance about my anger. This is a new life for me, and the things we experience from God can bring a new life for all.

GREAT INSIGHTS!

I started to write a Christmas letter for my son and daughter, and then I stopped and asked God to give me some insights about what I should write. Instantly he revealed that I should communicate my love to them. I was teary-eyed the whole time I wrote it, and also the three times I reread it before putting it into an envelope.

You Are Both Deeply Loved

I want to let you know that I am more delighted now with you both than I have ever been! As I think over your whole lives, I am so thankful for where I am with you both, and I am looking forward to your lives and your impact on those around you. I think and believe it will be far greater than any of us are aware.

Being your dad is the most important thing to me because I have learned what love is all about. Love is not primarily a feeling; it is a commitment. In my case, I am committed to love you day in and day out, all day long, over and over, no matter what is happening for good or ill. It is the way God says he loves us. He promised it and is committed to it. His love has amazed me, and my love toward the two of you has proved to me that God's love was a real influence on me.

I suppose it is natural that I may feel better when something works to the good. But my love for you both is not based on things working toward the good. It is a choice and a commitment. And I know it's real because I have had struggles with both of you (and you both have had struggles with me). And yet my love for you is unconditional. The struggles we have had prove that God's love is in me. I love you at a newer and higher level now compared to when you were both young.

God's love keeps us on the right path. I have experienced it toward me, even amid all my failures! There is nothing I could say or do to lose God's love. And there is nothing you could say or do to lose mine. No matter what, you are still loved. Thank God I experienced his love in a real way, and that is why my love for the two of you is so real.

I love you both more than anyone on planet Earth! That is no exaggeration. There is no one who loves you both at the depth that I do. Not even the love of wives and husbands or of parents and children can match the love I have for you.

I hope you both come to believe and remember that what I have said is genuine and true.

I love you! Your Dad

I trust my understanding of God's love has a good influence on my son and daughter. I hope it brings a new life to them, as it has for me.

PERSONALITIES INFLUENCE LIFE

I Have Two Personalities

There is something I haven't described in much detail. It's my personalities—plural. We all have personalities. Most people have two. Some have one. Knowing about them makes it a bit easier to remember life patterns and patterns of strengths and weaknesses. I have two personalities, the first one is called *sanguine* or *expressive*. There are other names for each personality based on the tests measuring them like DISC or Myers-Briggs.

The sanguine personality is about having fun and enjoying life, no matter what is going wrong. I have had fun even when things with my wife weren't working out or my goals with my children weren't achieved. Sanguine personalities tend to ignore bad things to concentrate on having fun. The downside of focusing on fun is what caused me to take so long to learn about my failures and what my part of the problem was. Fun was my personality priority, but it became boring compared to what I have experienced from God's promises of joy!

Joy is one of God's promises to us in the gospel of John:

> I tell you the truth, you will weep and mourn while the world rejoices. You will grieve, but your grief will turn to joy. A woman giving birth to a child has pain because her time has come; but when her baby is born she forgets the anguish because of her joy that a child is born into the world. So with you: Now is your time of grief, but I will see you again and you will rejoice, and no one will take away your joy. In that day you will no longer ask me anything. I tell you the truth, my Father will give you whatever you ask in my name. Until now you have not asked for anything in my name. Ask and you will receive, and your joy will be complete. (16:20–24)

For me the experience of joy was beyond fun. Even grief turned to joy, and joy became a real experience during my life's bad events. But I didn't have to ignore my problems to experience joy, not the way I had to ignore things to experience fun. Depending on your personality, fun may not be a priority. Regardless of your personality, joy is a major life emotion that everyone loves experiencing.

My second personality style is called *choleric* or *driver*. The choleric personality wants to be in control and to make things happen in record time. Most cholerics like telling people what to do and how to get it done—right now. The downside of wanting to make things happen is that controlling people is not the same as influencing and motivating them to do something the way they can do it. Influencing and motivating are much better than controlling.

Understanding My Weaknesses

The sanguine and choleric personality styles represent who I am and how I am. They can be good or bad. I was not aware of the negative outcomes for a long time because my lifestyle was so natural and comfortable, it kept me from being open to new insights into my personality. The strengths of those personalities became weaknesses because my strengths were exaggerated and I went out of bounds. We all need to be aware of our strengths becoming weaknesses. Your own personality style can make you feel comfortable about what and how you do things, but events may not be working out the way you hoped. That happened to me.

I loved having a fun life, but I enjoyed fun so much that this strength prevented me from understanding my weaknesses. My choleric personality wants to influence people, but I can go out of bounds when trying to control everything and everyone.

Because I learned about my problems, the strengths of my sanguine and choleric personalities are now influenced by God, and these traits are providing positive outcomes. Now I don't want to control others, and I am not expecting everything to work out within the deadlines I used to mandate. Now what I want to control are my mind and heart, not others. That is the way my personality can be more influential and less controlling.

A Recent New Life Experience at Work

I was recently training a group of new household salespeople. These people focus on selling just the materials required in homes, not companies or industries. The four concepts I teach in this class are 1.) how to prioritize a customer's needs and concerns; 2.) how to use our perspectives from a customer's point of view; 3.) how to stand on a narrow path and not become passive or aggressive; and 4.) how to step into chaos instead of running away from it or getting run over by it. The whole class got a chance to see me practice what I was teaching.

I stood in the middle path of a difficult event that one of the students caused, and I was treated badly by that student. He was a salesperson who had previously worked for a competitor. There was also a new sales supervisor in the class. Both made negative comments quite openly during my training. I could tell by the expressions of the others in the class that they were all very uncomfortable. Despite the problems I had with these two people, I remained at peace during the session and free of my old patterns. I enjoyed the whole week, even though these two were a problem.

What I Say Goes!

The group was wondering how I would handle the interruptions. I was tempted to tell the two they were being stupid. But in my heart I knew I should take their negative comments and deal with them in a way that would influence the whole group in a positive way to prove the concepts I was teaching. Remembering the exposure of my old patterns helped me stay on the right path of wanting to influence, rather than just react.

The first person I dealt with was the previous competitor. He told the class what to do about using something, and what he said was just not correct. So I told the group that was not what we would do.

He disagreed in an arrogant way.

I knew he was off track and was trying to control me and impress the group. So I reflected on what was said and asked him for the reasons he thought what he did.

What was said was still off track, so I told the group again that it was not what we will allow.

The person then made a sarcastic remark about me. The bad news is that I made a more sarcastic remark about him. I then closed off discussion by telling everyone that I was the national sales trainer and what I said goes!

Immediately I realized I had just handled things the wrong way—though what I said was totally accurate and I had authority to say what I did. I became uncomfortable with my sarcasm, but I had to continue the session. Lunch hour would be coming soon. When we broke for lunch, everyone left the room. As that person was walking out, I asked him to stay and talk with me for a few minutes. I was committed to stepping into the chaos, and I wanted to do it the right way.

We sat and talked. At the start it was very awkward. The person was arrogant and aggressive toward me, and I said we needed to walk through this concept and resolve it to avoid a bad outcome. I told him that if the director of training had been in the class, he would have been fired immediately for what he said and for trying to usurp authority over our salespeople.

He realized I was trying to be helpful when I said I wanted to walk through this, just between the two of us, and that I was not going to tell anyone about what happened. I wanted to work this out for both of our benefits. Then I apologized for being sarcastic in front of the group. I told him what I did was wrong and I asked his forgiveness.

He was shocked at how genuine I was about my part of the problem. After I admitted my fault, he immediately said he was the problem and expressed sorrow for what he had done. He said he had been a control freak all his life, and that he was grateful for the way I was handling this.

"I am excited with your candor," I said, "and I trust you will be the kind of salesperson we would love having in the company."

Then he admitted he "could still struggle with this kind of attitude."

I said we are all in the same boat, and the things I was teaching were critical for all of us to remember. It is most important for a great salesperson to be open to learning about our problems and controlling our thoughts and motives.

We shook hands and left. The rest of the week I had no problems with this person.

The process I used was effective because I remained aware of my old patterns. I had control of my thoughts toward the person, and I had faith that no matter what was wrong, God would use me to influence people in a good way.

Struggling with the Data

My next problem was with the lady who was a sales supervisor. We had different takes on a piece of technical information. What made things awkward was that she kept openly criticizing the data and saying it was all wrong. Almost every person talked to her about my concept before I had a chance to offer my opinion. She was objecting very loudly, and her tone was highly critical.

Having already stepped into a problem with the other person, I was committed to stay on the right path with this one. I would listen to what she was saying and try repeating it back to her to make sure I heard her correctly. But no matter what I said, it never connected.

Others would interrupt me and try to explain what I was saying, but she never got it.

I kept my tone, facial expression, and body language friendly. I even stood close to her so she would know I was listening. But this only made it worse.

She asked why I was attacking her. She perceived my standing close as an attack, and she started saying loudly that I was obviously mad at her. From her perspective, I was saying, "I think you are stupid, and I'm going to prove how stupid you are to the entire class."

Yet that was the furthest thing from my mind. I stepped toward her so she would know I was listening and trying to understand what she was saying. My only interest was in addressing her concerns. I knew she was really struggling with the data, and I wanted to help her figure it out.

I suggested we move on and handle the issue at another time. She was very unhappy and said, "Fine. Just move on!"

Stepping into Chaos

The day after the dustup with the sales supervisor, as we were headed out for lunch I asked her if we could spend some time together to talk about our disagreement and see if we could work things out. We sat out in a lounge and talked, but she was still furious at me and yelled so loudly that everyone in the lounge was looking at us.

She went through a half dozen comments about why I was the problem in that I didn't listen, didn't think right, didn't care for anyone else's opinion, and didn't teach things the way they needed to be taught.

I listened very carefully, then calmly repeated what she said. I told her I certainly wanted to be open to learning, and I asked if we could go back to the training room to talk about this because everyone in the lounge was listening to us.

She said, "No, let's stay here. I will talk softer." But that never happened. In fact her words became louder and nastier.

I listened to the same charges at least three more times, and no matter how clearly I repeated what was said, she would interrupt me and say it all again.

Standing in the Neutral Zone

As this continued, my heart focused on what causes someone to get this stuck on problems. I remembered when I had been this way, and I started feeling sorrow instead of anger. I wondered what was going on in her life to cause so much strife.

The sales supervisor kept repeating everything, and each time she would get even madder. For whatever reason, I became more at peace as the situation got worse! As I experienced this, I began thanking God for having brought about such real changes in my life to stop me from being centered on my problems.

I then told the supervisor something that had nothing to do with the topic from the class. I explained what I had struggled with in life about learning, listening, and what my mind was now doing to control my feelings and reactions when things went wrong. I talked about my struggles and what I learned about the Event Wheel concept and the Narrow Path concept that I teach in all my classes.

I was in a neutral zone, and I did not feel I needed to keep talking or try to make all this work out. It was clear she was struggling deeply with some life issues over which I had no control or influence. It even seemed that at the end of our discussion, she was more irritated than when we began.

I let her know that if she needed to leave the class and take it another time, or with someone else, she had my permission.

The next day her sales director showed up and pulled me aside. He told me this person had experienced some major life issues with an ex-spouse and a child, and that her job was a disaster right now because of all the changes happening in her life. That made total sense to me and made me grateful I had stood on that narrow path and stepped into the chaos!

The class observed what happened with the salesperson and the sales supervisor, and I heard good comments from students about how I handled those two people. For the rest of the week the first person contributed a good deal to the class. He brought insights, excitement about having a new job, and the experience of what he learned from his previous job.

My interaction with the second person, however, did not seem to help either her or me. She was still off track in her attitude about everything. Although I was tempted to become angry, irritated, or embarrassed because of her criticism, I didn't keep replaying the negative thoughts. I had to trust that my heart was in the right place. Though I did not win the day with her, I was glad to have walked through both negative events with the class in a way that was helpful for everyone.

When students see me living the way I teach, that works to their good. Over my years of training, in most classes I have had difficulties with one or two students. When I handle that on the narrow path, I get a lot of positive comments from students who tell me they find what I teach is life-changing.

I feel good about doing this as a trainer because it proves the concepts I teach for salespeople to use with their customers.

New Desires

I can still get angry, but I don't want to anymore. In fact, now I hate it when I get angry. And if I get angry at someone else, I always have to remember that I was once like them. I have been where they have been, and I have done what they have done. And I have learned that God loves us all. Now that I understand about being loved by God and loving God, I am way more able to actually love others—even when they don't love me back or don't treat me decently. It frees me from my old patterns and gives me new desires.

REMEMBER TO LEARN FROM PAIN AND THE PRICE OF PAIN

Remembering Earlier Lessons

I first became open to God exposing things about me to get me on the right track when my son was fourteen and doing drugs. I realized that although he was responsible for his behavior, I had influenced what he chose to do. I knew that if I didn't experience a real change in my heart, I could never influence my son and family in the best way. I wanted to love my son instead of trying to fix him, control him, or expect him to do what I wanted.

My thought patterns began changing. Instead of what I needed or wanted, I became more interested in what my family needed. I learned to admit things in a new way. I began sharing the issues I struggled with to my friends. I also talked about my personal problems at work or church. Admitting my weaknesses to others helped me focus on my perspectives and opinions and helped me figure out what was wrong with me. It makes sense why the Bible tells us to confess to each other

(James 5:16). Remembering the pain I had caused my family helped me to confess my shortcomings.

You Can't Fix Yourself

I thought that controlling my anger would bring about change. When things went wrong between my wife and me, I tried not to react and do the same things I had done in the past—cussing, yelling, threatening, or walking away from her. There were times when I didn't get angry as quickly as I used to. It seemed I was making a change, but that change was not coming quickly enough.

The longer it took for me to get angry, the more truth was exposed about my staying the same and not changing. I would still blow up, and when I blew up, it was way worse! The energy I used trying to fix myself caused me to get even angrier. Then guilt would attack me because I could not control my anger. I tried every way possible to fix myself. I had never in my life poured so much energy into sin management and behavioral control. A friend who was my counselor said he had never seen anyone try to change anger for as long as I did.

I was so frustrated that I couldn't change my pattern of getting angry that I finally came upon a new thought: I cannot fix myself.

Was my good intention to fix my anger useless? Nope! It caused more damage, guilt, excuses, and judgment of others, and for years it wasted a pile of time in my life. The pain and the price of that pain finally brought about the good news that change can come—when it comes from the inside out. Admitting I couldn't fix myself opened the gate for new solutions and better intentions.

Exposed in My Car

Something happened at a church meeting that would have made many people mad. At the time, I thought I handled it well. A friend said that my response was good and that I did not seem angry, but that I "might want to ponder what was going on in my mind."

Yet within seconds of leaving the parking lot, I was exploding mentally and emotionally. I was cussing, calling people names, and thinking I would never go to that church again or talk to any of those people about anything I plan to do. I screamed in my mind for about five miles. And I became physically nauseated! Though I responded well in front of the group and did not explode during the meeting, I was definitely infuriated. My best friend was the pastor of the church, yet I was so angry I was ready to quit going there.

What became clear while driving from the church was that my thoughts were wiping me out. I had judged those people as if I had never done what they did to me! One elder had said my thoughts and plans were bad and would not work. They also said that they were not even going to read my program because they knew it would not work. Another agreed with that and wondered why I hadn't figured out all the financial outcomes and that until I did, they didn't want to deal with this.

I remembered when I had displayed similar attitudes and had shut down people with my rude comments. I realized that even though they had hurt me, I had to be open to discover what my part was.

So I went through the concept process that's listed at the start of this section. It took me about three months to work through it all. That became another experience of change. Fortunately, I got healed more quickly from the church meeting because of all I had learned years ago about my lifestyle.

GETTING TO THE ROOTS

In an earlier chapter I told the story of the critical hiker at Arches National Park. That was one experience about the core patterns of exposure, insights, connecting the dots, the process of healing and change, and having faith in God. Because we are free of accusation from God, I don't need to put my own or anyone else's accusations between myself and God. Discovering root issues helps maintain new life experiences and prevents things from keeping us stuck in a rut.

What, How, and Why

Getting to the roots of my problems has helped me experience a new type of life. Exposure to my problems revealed what was happening, and the fact that I was starting to pay attention to *what* was happening helped the *how* and *why* become more evident. It became obvious that the *how* and *why* were more important than the *what*. The *what* just represented symptoms, but the path to the root was the *how* and *why*.

I can discover answers at any time. I didn't always realize that, but now it is obvious that almost every day, at any time, I have a chance to learn not only what and how I am thinking, but also what I am doing that I should not be, and what I am not doing that I should be.

To discover how things go wrong, I need to stop using my preconceived opinions and open myself to new insights. Learning *how* I did something is easier and quicker than focusing on *why* I did something. Discovering the *why* of a thing can take a long time and may require outside help. Because that is true, getting at the *why* should be one's last priority.

If I replay a negative thought, that is how I make myself angry, aggressive, fearful, worried, or passive. If I forget, I talk too much and keep doing it, which is how I keep others from wanting to listen. When I try to control others, that is how I keep making them angry. Every day when something happens, I want to consider what I did and how I came to do it that way. This really gives me insights, for good or bad.

More Pieces of the Puzzle

The "what" piece of the puzzle has to do with outward symptoms or inward feelings. Outward symptoms are easier for me to realize because they are usually displayed on my face. Feelings come from thoughts, and negative feelings come from negative thoughts. The problem with the question of what went wrong is that I can focus on changing the symptoms instead of the core cause. Typically my thoughts about the *how* and *why* were off track and not true insights because I had judged people. When I realized I had done the same things that I judge others for, I wondered about my motives.

The "why" piece of the puzzle is the hardest and takes the longest to discover. When I had an inaccurate opinion about why someone did something, I judged them wrongly. And I did the same thing to myself. My opinions about why I did things were off track because they came from reactions to things from long ago—like those early life events that wounded my soul. Some I had forgotten with time. Whenever I had strong opinions, I closed my mind toward hearing and believing other perspectives. I thought, for example, that I knew my wife and why she did what she did to make me angry. But I did not know her, and I was always wrong about her reasons.

Why did I go down the wrong path so often? Because I replayed negative concepts over and over in my mind. This created negative feelings that caused negative reactions. I can find accurate answers to the *why* question only by being open to asking others, reconsidering my thoughts, praying for insights, and going back into my history to discover why I did things. I am sure there are still things I don't remember, but I am more at peace and I know I am now on the right path for change. (Go back to page 138 and look at my Big If" for helpful tips about changes.)

Blind Spots and Deaf Spots

I used to think I was willing to learn a lot. Then I discovered I was mainly interested in learning only what I wanted to learn or what I already agreed with. Most of us know the concept about blind spots—where one does not see things plainly. But what about "deaf spots"? Ears pick up only what we want to hear—and shut out what we don't want to hear. I was a master at that! That was one reason why I kept screwing up my intentions, beliefs, lifestyle, attitudes, expectations, problems, hopes, and dreams. My arrogance kept me from learning many things, and that arrogance came from judging others. I was blind and deaf to it, and it caused a large gap in my life. Here is an example:

A Life Gap the Size of the Grand Canyon

I dreamed that my children would see me as a great dad who loved them deeply. I still have these desires! My wish to be a great dad triggered what I thought were good intentions to help them. I expected, in turn, that they would appreciate me and honor me for what I tried to do for them. I gave them directions and rules about what to do and what not to do, and I did this for their own good.

When they didn't show appreciation and obedience for my guidance, I was disappointed and frustrated. So I would repeat my directions. Then my kids would show disinterest, and I would start applying pressure about what they needed to do. Reacting to the pressure, they would resent me. I would then make demands and threats—and the whole situation would unravel. It was never what I hoped would happen.

Still, I remained committed to the best results, which meant controlling my children in order to help them. When their needs and wants did not align with mine, I would still expect them to do things my way because I thought I was being wiser.

I was blinded to my problems because of my good intentions. I believed that my children were the ones who needed to learn, not me! This does not mean that I had nothing good and appropriate to teach them. All of our children need to learn some obvious things from their parents. But I was focused on my perspectives and priorities—with all their blind spots and deaf spots. Was I clueless!

I thought that if I just kept doing what I had been doing, they would eventually understand my reasoning and see things my way. Then they would appreciate me for having helped them. So I repeated the same things over and over. I did this with my wife as well, because my intention was to be a great husband.

On a scale of 1 to 10 (with 10 being disastrous), others may see our issues at an 8, 9, or 10, while we may see them at 3, 4, or 5. The gap of truth between our perspective and others' could be the size of the Grand Canyon. Trust me, that gap was my part of the problem.

Something Exciting

There is some good news about knowing all that was wrong with me. Admitting my mistakes and weaknesses no longer embarrasses me. In fact, I enjoy telling people what was wrong with me because my life experiences can help others. I can't fake my current comfort, joy, freedom, and peace. How could I ever be so candid about myself if I faked those things? My stories are aimed at people whose lives are like mine and my children's.

The next Christmas story offers more proof.

ANOTHER GREAT CHRISTMAS DAY

About forty years after becoming a follower of Christ, I wrote this in my journal:

Thursday, Christmas Morning

It's Thursday, Christmas morning, and I am journaling today about my life since I became a Christian. I think today is a good opportunity to reflect on the many changes in my life. Lately I've been getting more insights about our four basic needs of being loved and loving others, self-worth, significance, and security. The Bible is clear that God wants to fill our hearts and minds with those things. For me, believing I am loved by God needs to be my life foundation.

When I became a believer I experienced God's love. Over time, however, his love for me was forgotten because I was focused on my negative events and feelings. My four basic needs were not being met due to some personal accusations from others that drained my heart and mind.

I had some internal patterns of fighting back at accusations and accusing those who threw them at me. I would justify my actions and think I had saved myself from their assaults. Many years later I realized those accusations and assaults had caused internal wounds and that my heart was not healed from those wounds. I thought I had minimized, excused, justified, and explained away those things. But I was using my negative thoughts to repeatedly tell myself how screwed up others were. I was judging others, but I was unaware of the negative effects judging caused within me.

I spent a lot of time and energy focusing on those negative thoughts, which caused feelings of bitterness, resentment, and anger. The feelings brought out of my mouth sarcasm, slander, and ridicule. Sometimes I pretended I was fine and wouldn't say anything negative, but in my heart there was a lot of anger.

As a Christian I read the Bible a lot and gained some good intellectual knowledge about the faith. With that knowledge I thought I was a good Christian. I didn't realize that experiencing the knowledge was the key factor! A few years before the divorce I realized something about the outward symptoms of my life. I was not having a helpful influence on my family, and the scarier part was that I was not having a good influence on my son. It struck me that if my life was going to have a positive impact on my son, then it had to change in a very real way. If it didn't, he would see through the façade of my so-called Christian lifestyle.

I now realize how tangible God's love for me is. I haven't had a wife or a girlfriend in many years (I've only dated once in ten years), and yet I have never felt so loved. I have not experienced any loneliness at all. When bad things happen, there is no denying the peace within my life. I am not perfect and never will be, but there is more daily joy in my life than I have ever experienced before. When assaults and accusations came during the divorce, there was hurt and frustration because the accusations were false. But I was able to quickly let go of those thoughts. Then peace, joy, and love toward my wife took over my heart—even during the divorce.

It was so real to me. It was like the kingdom of heaven actually came down and took over my life. My friends got to see, hear, and experience my peace, joy, and love toward others and myself. I have written about it all in my journals over the last ten years, and I have reread it repeatedly so I would not forget what God has done for me and how he loves me.

Right now while writing this portion in my journal, things in my life aren't where I would have liked them to be. My son is having a hard time. He is without work, and it seems at some level he is feeling shame, guilt, and discomfort due to his past. I suspect he may feel he isn't measuring up to either his standards or mine. But I also suspect he knows he is not measuring up to God's standard. But he is trying to make life work. He is likely to be on the same path I was on when I wasn't meeting my own good intentions or meeting others' expectations of me.

Our relationship is not where I hoped it would be, and it seems my son is no more open to hearing about things from me than I was about hearing things from others. Regardless, I am delighted I get to love him while he lives with me. As I consider all that happened in his life and mine, my love for him is a commitment that does not depend on his lifestyle with me. It is about hope and love, not about expectations.

I had very important plans and visions of things I thought would take place in the last year. But they haven't come about. There also was a meeting at my church that caused an incredibly deep wound in me, but at least I got to see something about myself that revealed an emotional wound I have had for over thirty-five years. I was able to come to a place of insight and be released from not only the pain, but also from the old wounds in the past and the attitudes about it that were hidden within me. I feel freer than ever.

Financially I may be at risk. Some things happened that sent me to the hospital four times in the last year. Not to mention that the national economy has tanked, so the company I work for is letting lots of people go. Tomorrow there is a meeting that might reveal I am being let go, yet I am not concerned. It hasn't crossed my mind to look for a job right away. I believe God provided this job, and I do not need to panic over things I cannot control!

My daughter called last Monday and described a horrible experience where someone assaulted her verbally. What she told me had the potential of taking me down the wrong path, and it would have some time ago. But this time it didn't, and I helped her walk through what happened and get free of the accusations thrown at her. I was comfortable and peaceful and had no accusation against the person who attacked my daughter in this way. It was my ex-wife! After talking with my daughter about it, she was amazed at my attitude and it helped her stay on the right path toward her mother. She told me she knew I had been healed of rage and bitterness, and she wanted to be healed of them also.

This Christmas will be spent with friends again for the tenth year. I have not been with my family for Christmas since the divorce. I love hanging with my friends and it is always a delight, but every Christmas I hope to enjoy my children, the way my friends enjoy theirs.

Kari still lives in Arizona because during the divorce my wife took my daughter with her. My daughter's new family lives there, and it is hard for me to get there to see them very often. We do talk a lot on the phone. I wish we could spend more time together, but I am grateful for what has been redeemed between her family and me. And as I sit here and write, my eyes are watery and I am having trouble seeing because of my tears.

None of it is from sorrow! It is my heart's delight in how my life is and how delighted it makes me because of the freedom I have from my old lifestyle. And it is from the joy, gratitude, and peace that I have in my life now. I cannot think of any major area of my life that is working the way I hoped or wanted it to, except for the spiritual side of things. Even so, I am on solid ground right now with my faith toward God. I love my life and am filled to the brim with joy and love toward the Creator. If I weren't at home now with my son sleeping upstairs, there would be wailing and howling in delight at how loved and cared for I am! I love life because my connection with God is so real.

About five minutes after writing this, a thought came to me. It was God saying, "Merry Christmas. This is your gift from me."

PUTTING IT ALL TOGETHER

What are the odds that my parents and all the others I have complained about wanted to be bad people and do the wrong things? The odds are very long, even though I experienced wounds from them and felt they were controlling me and using me to meet their own expectations. Not only was I using everyone in my life to try to get my needs met, but I also lived in a conflict of interest with everyone around me because I was serving only myself. I spent my time trying to fulfill my needs and expected others to fulfill them also. I was blind to my motives because, in my mind, my intentions were so good. Putting others' negative judgments about me between me and God caused a serious problem. When I discovered these insights about my life problems, they all made sense.

A New View on Life

In the gospel of Luke we read that Christ exposes the thoughts of our hearts: "The thoughts of many hearts will be revealed. And a sword will pierce your own soul too" (2:35). John's gospel makes it clear that God provides light to reveal the truth about our lives: "Everyone who does evil hates the light, and will not come into the light for fear that his deeds will be exposed. But whoever lives by the truth comes into the light, so that it may be seen plainly that what he has done has been done through God" (3:20–21). Finding out what was going on inside me was a key factor in my transition and transformation. One thing that helped me gain a new perspective on life was that I gave my friends permission to speak openly and candidly to me about anything.

It took a long time for me to come to the place of wanting my personal problems revealed. But I was becoming more and more open and willing to consider things I hadn't thought of, or things that might have indicated I was on the wrong track. That attitude allowed for change, and I developed the habit of spending time with others discussing my life's issues to build a foundation of insights, vulnerability, and honesty. I was relieved to think there might be a way out of this dilemma as I revealed myself to others and to God.

The Heart Path

Experiencing forgiveness was another step in exposing the thoughts of my heart. It was encouraging that my friends forgave me for my faults and continued hanging out with me. I expected them to give up on me. Their forgiveness also gave me a tangible picture of the Bible's teaching about God's forgiveness of us. The more that was revealed about my life, the more I understood and experienced forgiveness. It freed me to look forward to seeing my part in the problems that were evident in my life. Not only did I want to stop doing the wrong things, but I also needed and wanted to experience forgiveness. That made me want to forgive others also, because I realized I have done to others all the things that they have done to me.

All the name-calling had to stop. People I called idiots, morons, and whatever else, were no better or no worse than me. It became clear to me that I was losing the attitude that compelled me to call people offensive names. In fact, the week after I encountered the man at Arches National Park, I got a picture in my mind of running into him again and telling him the whole story about how God exposed me and used him to do it. I envisioned us both laughing and apologizing to each other.

Forgiving has also made me more willing to stand with someone in a personal problem instead of attacking them or running away. Since I do not let my negative thoughts control me, I do not get run over by events. All this helped me want to stop judging others and to avoid people who do things that tempt me to react. I am learning to stand in the middle path.

In *Wild at Heart: Discovering the Secret of a Man's Soul,* author John Eldredge calls what I am describing "the heart path." The heart path makes some sense to me now. There is a fascinating verse in the book of Ephesians about standing firm and doing battle in life: "Therefore put on the full armor of God, so that when the day of evil comes, you may be able to stand your ground, and after you have done everything, to stand, stand firm then ..." (6:13, 14). Standing firm prevents the fight and flight responses and the aggressive and passive reactions. Do I always stand firm? No, I am never perfect, but I stand firmer now than I ever have.

Big or Little Butt Kickers

Little things cause more problems for me now than the big ones did. We may all be in the same boat. Many of us get through catastrophic difficulties. But the little things that happen to us all day, every day, annoy us to no end. They irritate us, cause us to become impatient, make us complain, frustrate us, and lead us to despair. They take us down the wrong path toward bad attitudes and blaming everyone for our problems.

We all have our list of irritating butt kickers. Here are some of mine: Driving in town and hitting all the red lights. Standing in a long line at the grocery store. Getting sales calls on my cell phone. My neighbor's dogs barking all day. People interrupting me during presentations and conversations at work. My internet service not working. My computer getting stuck.

Although I had a new view of life because of big events, I got even more insights for walking through the daily small things. Everyone regularly experiences these little butt kicking events. It is the little bitty butt kickers that continue exposing me and revealing what takes me down the wrong path. Those things happen every day, and whenever they happen I need to battle to control my negative thoughts—something I will have to do for the rest of my life.

All the concepts I have discussed can heal me of these little butt kickers. There are steps to each one. For example, the concept of controlling my attitude by not replaying negative thoughts. When I get a negative thought, it is much easier to keep repeating it instead of letting it go or fighting against it. I have assumed such thoughts would go away because I knew about the concept of not replaying negative thoughts. Yet I was still replaying them. So I remembered I really do have to battle the thoughts, and sometimes that takes hours. The worst events that create the most negative thoughts can take days. Now I do battle more often than not, and that puts me at a great advantage.

I have gotten through battles both large and small, and I can guarantee that battling against negative things and gaining peace and freedom is a real experience! Especially when you are committed to taking the effort to control negative thoughts.

New Motives

God exposed my old motives, and now I have gained new ones. Although it is tempting to have wrong motives, I am more aware of the outcomes if I get stuck on negative paths. When I set my mind on positive thoughts I experience feelings of peace and joy, and I gain freedom from my old style. My new set of motives is to be committed to love, help, serve, and honor others. My motives going forward in life promise an adventure.

I look forward to life because every year I get closer to God. Life is exciting. Although things didn't work the way I expected, I feel I am on the path God wanted me on, and it is certainly the path I want to be on. Though on occasion things still hit the fan, life is generally peaceful and joyful, and it no longer takes me down the toilet.

The rest of my life story is still to come. I don't know what it will bring, but exploring what is going on inside me will keep the transformation going.

EXPERIENCING GOD'S KINGDOM

There are three important Scriptures about experiencing God's kingdom. The first one is Matthew 6:33, which says, "Seek first his kingdom and his righteousness, and all these things will be given to you as well." Jesus said we will gain the things we need if we first seek the kingdom and God's righteousness. The key factor here is seeking.

The second Scripture is Acts 14:22: "We must go through many hardships to enter the kingdom of God." This has to do with experiencing the kingdom of God on earth and confronting life's events, not running away from them. Standing on the middle path with faith in God means going through hardship.

Colossians 3:1–2 is the third Scripture. It reads, "Since, then, you have been raised with Christ, set your hearts on things above, where Christ is seated at the right hand of God. Set your minds on things above, not on earthly things." This relates to the Event Wheel concept of controlling our thoughts and focusing on heavenly things rather than the world's concepts.

Remembering what is good is so important, that in the Old Testament books of Genesis and Exodus, God told people to tell good stories to their children and their children's children, and to place pillars of rocks where God's interventions took place so the people could be reminded every time they passed. And when they passed, they were to tell everyone the story of what happened. God said this was so they would remember him and what he had done. Furthermore, he told the Hebrew people to do it forever. As we remember the good, we experience God's kingdom in our lives.

I can't build pillars all over the nation. So writing and re-reading my journals helps me remember the good things God has done in my life. I go back to my journal about every three months. Once a year I go back through the whole year's accounts. I do whatever it takes to trigger good memories. In my journals I record events, thoughts, feelings, reactions, and insights—whatever comes to me. I even write about negative things, because they remind me of what I want to change. I never forget God's promise "that in all things God works for the good of those who love him, who have been called according to his purpose" (Romans 8:28). My life's stories prove that is real!

Inward Healing

For me, experiencing God's kingdom meant laying myself wide open to learning what was wrong with me. How had I gotten into negative patterns? Why did I always want to judge people? Insights revealed a pattern about my symptoms. I needed to be healed inwardly instead of trying to control the outward actions.

I made a life commitment to spend time reading, writing, praying, and talking to a couple of friends about my Christian life. I would do these regularly so that they became habits. And I made very practical changes, such as going to bed earlier so I could get up early and start my days reading the Bible, using my journal to write about my thoughts, and connecting the dots. Connecting to God in prayer and reading helpful Christian books provided a positive influence for the day.

While I experienced positive life events, all too often I forgot them. Instead, remembering the negatives became my emotional fuel. It was easier to remember and replay the negatives, and this kept me stuck in a rut. Becoming aware of that helps me let go of them—and to remember and replay the positives. But letting go of negative thoughts is still a battle.

Sometimes when I thought I was "fixed," I didn't stay open to additional perspectives. I didn't think I needed any more change because I was fine! But I was unaware of deeper issues. Eventually, I did remember that God and my friends were trying to get through to me.

Controlling thought patterns is a key to inner healing. Realizing I was thinking negatively—and was stuck on replaying those thoughts—helped me focus on positive ideas. It is obvious to me now that I need to maintain the foundational pattern of remembering the positives, replaying them, and believing the truth of how my past stories have worked out. It has been more than a decade since I learned that, and it is one of the most helpful things I deal with daily. And I realize this must remain one of my priorities for the rest of my life.

Healed from the Inside Out

Experiencing the kingdom of God on earth is also about real healing. I used to assume I could control my outward behaviors. My experiences proved me wrong. What I needed was a heart change. My anger, which was rooted in expectations that others would do what I wanted and needed, was one of my faults that had to be healed from the inside out. My heart change came when I realized that everyone struggles with the same problems. Coming to terms with that helped heal me of anger toward others.

I wanted to be a great dad and husband. I needed my wife and children to make me feel that I was really succeeding in those areas. I wanted to be great at my job, and I needed my boss to treat me that way. I wanted to be a great Christian, and while I was not treated as such by some church leaders, I still wanted to be on the right path.

Those were some of my thought patterns. But I discovered that everyone else was in the same boat. They all wanted me to meet their expectations and needs. Yet I could no more meet their needs all the time than they could meet mine. Even the people who loved me had done things that hurt me. There was a mutual conflict of interest between me and everyone. Seeing things this way was a good start for healing, but it did not provide the solution.

Faith in God's Love for Me

The solution to inward healing and to stop controlling my outward behavior was a change of heart. And that came from faith in God's love for me in spite of all my shortcomings. It allowed me to see that I was like those I hurt or was hurt by. That helped me stop judging them and expecting them to be perfect in meeting all my needs.

Focusing on how much God loved me helped me remember to start loving myself. Then I started experiencing peace—even about things that did not work out. I started loving others more like the way God loved me. Peace became my overriding emotion, and it healed my anger. Over the years, my anger has almost disappeared, especially compared to my past. But because anger was a major pattern of my life for so long, I still struggle against negative thoughts. I probably will for the rest of my life.

Life on this planet is not perfect for anyone. For many, it is not even good. For some, it is a continual disaster. But those connected to God can experience his kingdom on earth.

I have found two books that are very helpful about the concepts of our thoughts: *Escaping the Matrix* by Greg Boyd and *Inside Out* by Larry Crabb. I have read each at least three times. They are very good writers, and their books detail concepts that are outstanding in influencing any of us for some real changes.

MY NEW LIFE EXPERIENCES

My faith in God has brought me through some hard lessons and has allowed me new experiences in all areas of my life.

Ian

My son and I have had opportunities to talk to men's groups at retreats about our stories. A group has even approached him about doing a movie based on the miracles in his life. Ian and the chief of police, who was part of the whole ordeal, have played basketball together. My son still lives with me, and I trust he is experiencing the love of God through his dad. I am getting to experience my intentions about loving my son! When his life goes down a new path, it has the potential to impact others' lives even more than mine.

Kari

My daughter remains very close to me, and she is a princess of delight to me and her family. We talk all the time, and sometimes we go on for hours on the phone. She has grown close to God and talks to me all the time about her spiritual experiences. I had the best intentions to be a great father, and now Kari sees me as that very person. She tells me regularly that I am her number one mentor!

Casen

My grandson is a special friend who calls me "Grandpa Colorado." When I spend time with him, he always asks why I love him so much. When I am at his home he hugs me, kisses me, sits on my lap, and spends more time with me than anyone else. God has given me a wonderful promise about what he will do with my grandson. When he was young the name he called me was Crap o rado. Yes, it was, and is hilarious! There may have been some truth!

Jason

My son-in-law has also become a close friend. We camp and get to spend other times together. I am getting to know him like a son. He remains open to learning from me about making his family life better, and I am thankful that I get to spend time with him and stay at his home. Having gone through our family's ups and downs, he wants to learn and grow. I am honored by him. The best part for me is observing how my daughter loves Jason and focuses on her issues with their marriage. She loves him to the fullness of her heart.

My Mom

Mom and I talk almost daily, and I love being her son. She is so encouraging to me and has made it clear that I have touched her life in a great way. She is so proud of me, which is something I never experienced from anyone when I was younger. She reveals her love to me repeatedly, which has had a great impact on my heart. She often tells me I have brought her closer to God and that I am her great encourager.

My Job

I am the North American national sales trainer for the corporation Culligan International, where I work. For the last eleven years I have had a personal impact on individuals in our company all across North America. I love my job! I have learned so much about influencing people with positive motives. I love working with my bosses, I get to help others become more comfortable with their bosses, and I get to see bosses becoming better influences on their employees!

My Town, Church, and Friends

I love where I live, in the beautiful mountains of Western Colorado in a place called Glenwood Springs, because of the people I experience life with. I have close friends with whom I connect all the time who have impacted my life in many positive ways. I go to a great nondenominational church, "The Orchard," where my best friend Doug Self is the pastor. But most of all, I really love my life because I have truly connected with God and I am free from being my old self.

My Hopes and Thoughts for Your New Life Experiences

The apostle Paul wrote, "We know that in all things God works for the good of those who love him, who have been called according to his purpose" (Rom. 8:28). My hope is that readers will find a relational connection with God that will bring about a new, better, deeper, and more exciting life-changing experience.

This is not about becoming religious or intellectual, but about experiencing who God is and how much he loves us. Remembering daily for the rest of your life how deeply loved you are will bring his love unconditionally to those in your life. I hope that what I learned may help others understand what keeps them from seeing and experiencing God at the level they want and need.

If you are a Christian but have not experienced the things you wanted, I hope this book provides insights to create a deep desire to let God expose you and reveal things to you. What he reveals will bring you new insights and a new lifestyle. Following Christ will take you to the fullest freedom and allow you to experience his love for you. His love for and through you will touch those you want to love.

But if you are not a Christian—and have not wanted to become one because of the hypocrisy of Christians or other negative experiences—I hope this book prompts a real desire to experience God. Ask him, as I did, to prove himself to you. I hope you will begin spiritual habits and commit your efforts toward finding faith in God. Starting that change and connecting to God is something you can control.

The Kingdom of God

"The time has come," the gospel of Mark tells us. "The kingdom of God is near. Repent and believe the good news" (1:15). God uses life's events for us to experience spiritual things in the kingdom of God. He provides the faith for us to withstand or walk through serious situations.

Most of the time when things don't work out for us, it is because we are preventing God from being a part of our lives. He will not nullify our free will. If we choose to avoid him, that is our prerogative. Avoiding him, however, puts us at serious risk in life's events. But when we live, walk, and stand in faith, even the worst events can eventually become the path into the kingdom of God and heaven on earth.

What brings the experience of the kingdom? In my case it was recovering from the losses I experienced. My list of losses may not compare to what others experience, but in the final analysis the losses I suffered caused me to experience peace, joy, comfort, freedom, and hope. They helped me realize how deeply God loves me.

I am now at a place where I love life, and the bad things that happened no longer bother me. To me, this is experiencing the kingdom of God. As Acts 14:22 says, "We must go through many hardships to enter the kingdom of God." The results of my hardships, and my learning to withstand bad events, helps me step into the chaos. This is a choice we must all make. Trusting that God is who he says he is—and does what he says he will do—puts us in the center of the battlefield and prepares us to battle hardships. Here is the way the apostle Paul puts it:

> Finally, be strong in the Lord and in his mighty power. Put on the full armor of God so that you can take your stand against the devil's schemes. For our struggle is not against flesh and blood, but against

the rulers, against the authorities, against the powers of this dark world and against the spiritual forces of evil in the heavenly realms. Therefore put on the full armor of God, so that when the day of evil comes, you may be able to stand your ground, and after you have done everything, to stand. Stand firm then, with the belt of truth buckled around your waist, with the breastplate of righteousness in place, and with your feet fitted with the readiness that comes from the gospel of peace. In addition to all this, take up the shield of faith, with which you can extinguish all the flaming arrows of the evil one. Take the helmet of salvation and the sword of the Spirit, which is the word of God. And pray in the Spirit on all occasions with all kinds of prayers and requests. With this in mind, be alert and always keep on praying for all the saints.

—Ephesians 6:10–18

God's Path

Because I have always been tempted to think negatively, I ask myself why I would walk down a negative mental path after all the events God has walked me through. So I choose to remember God's promises and the peace and joy that followed when he pulled me through the bad spots.

One of the very cool things I get to tell others is what my life was once like and what I did that caused so much failure. Though some of it had nothing to do with my faults, my experiences can help others understand and improve their lifestyles. We all experience failures, but as we walk with God on his path, it brings about successes in the spiritual realm. When we experience spiritual success, we go from the bad to the good, and from the good to the great. And we influence people in a significant way.

I hope and trust that my life stories will provide fruit for you—and that you will also experience a new and better life. The changes that bring a new life can happen to anyone who is open to these possibilities. I pray you will experience God's love for you!

This was supposed to be the end of the book. But during the week I was to send the manuscript to the publisher, another event took place. It is the most incredible story I have ever experienced! It is the postscript.

POSTSCRIPT:
A DEATH
BROUGHT NEW
LIFE

On Wednesday, September 22, 2010, my mom died. That week I was in Yuma, Arizona, staying at her house. I had remained at the hospital for hours Monday and Tuesday while she was unconscious. Many friends came in and prayed for her, and they were all very emotionally engaged.

Besides me, her stepdaughter and my brother's ex wife, both of whom Mom treated as her daughters, were at the hospital almost all day and even stayed overnight. Her pastor was there for hours each day, and he stayed in the hospital longer than anyone. I spent a lot of time at Mom's house on Monday and Tuesday, writing in my journal and pondering her life as I was preparing for some upcoming national webinars I would be conducting the following week.

Mom Might Die

I had gone to Arizona to hang out with Mom because she was having gall bladder surgery. None of us thought the operation would be serious, and no one expected her to die. Although she'd had a stroke about six months before, she seemed OK. The stroke had cost her some of her memory, but this seemed like the typical thing when people can't remember a few names and some things that happened long ago.

After the surgery, Mom was in a great mood. But within hours she began suffering severe pain, then lost consciousness. She opened her eyes a few times, but they did not work. She was not seeing anything, and she was struggling to breathe.

Now it became clear that she might die. Her family and friends knew what Mom's life was like—and how she was very comfortable about dying. She was God's child and believed what the Bible said about death and eternal life. But we were all heartbroken. We didn't want her to die.

Mom Died

I was staying at Mom's house because all her close friends were at the hospital. None of them wanted to lose her. I wanted her friends to be comfortable about whatever they were feeling, and I didn't want my being there to cause any issues. I did not know her friends well, because I hadn't lived in Arizona since 1975. I felt a bit nervous being there because I was her only child present.

But I was comfortable about my mother dying. She and I had talked about this for more than a year, and I knew where her mind and heart were about it all. At her age, she was happier about dying than staying alive. She said she knew that in heaven she would not have her severe arthritis, nor would she have the consequences of her stroke and liver problems.

On Wednesday morning at 6:15, my brother's ex-wife Kathy called me and said, "Mom just died." It took me five minutes to get to the hospital. When I got there, Kathy was crying. She said Mom had opened her eyes just before dying, and they knew she was seeing through them because her eyes had changed dramatically. She knew that Mom was looking at Jesus or heaven, because as her eyes opened, she was smiling. And then she died.

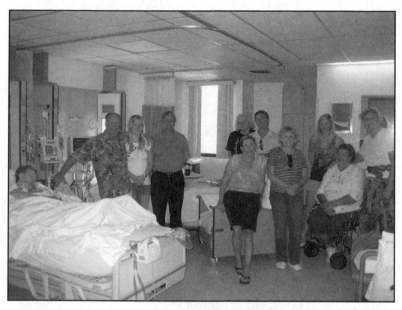

My mom and her friends with me before she died

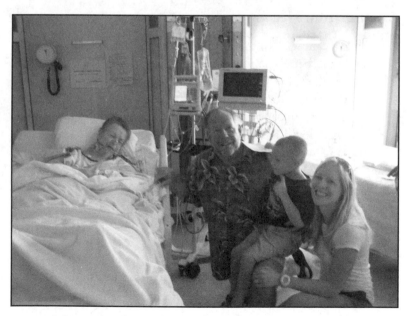

Me, my daughter and grandson with mom before she died

An Unusual Walk

I felt peace and a joy about my mom's death. I kissed her on the forehead and smiled. As others came to see her, I decided I would go for a long walk along a canal near the hospital. I wanted to spend time talking out loud to God. I didn't want to make her friends uncomfortable because I wasn't brokenhearted, so I left.

I was glad there was no one on the road when I started walking along the canal, because I began talking out loud to God about events that had happened early in my life between Mom and me. As I started talking, I was not at all mad, but I was recalling all the bad events and describing them out loud. I had never talked like this about them, and I didn't know why they were coming out now. But they kept coming. I went from when I was young up through my current age. Some of those things were terrible. As I described them, I got thoughts that clarified the past—and I began crying in delight, not sorrow! God was making it clear that he had used all of my past to bring me to him. This was a most unusual walk on a dirt road.

Insights from Heaven

While recalling all of these things, I came to the time I joined the Navy and then became a follower of Christ. More than ever before, it became evident that God used my mother to bring me to him, to change my heart, and to save my life. He had used my disastrous relationship with my mother to bring me into the kingdom. I will mention just one thing to illustrate.

I hated my mom so much that when I turned fourteen and could legally leave her, I did. That same day I also reported her to the police. My mom had threatened to kill me, and once she actually tried. When she threw a large pair of scissors at me it missed, but it stuck into the wall next to my heart where I was sitting at the table. Another time she tried to kill my young brother with a hatchet. I prevented it by using a broomstick to keep her from him. But I was afraid to tell the police about that stuff. So instead I lied and told them she had starved me and my brother, and we were leaving her.

I moved in with my dad and stepmom and brought my young brother with me. In that day, Mom lost her two sons. I didn't talk to her for five years. Right after I left, her heart was so broken and her thoughts were so negative, she started experiencing what turned into horribly severe arthritis. What I had done to her had probably triggered the arthritis, and her thoughts started to ruin her body. But on this walk God revealed to me that he had used what I had done in leaving her to bring my mother to him!

When I joined the Navy I became a Christian, and about three months later Mom also met Christ. Neither would have happened if I had not left home. When I was in Vietnam, I started writing letters to her—the first time I had written since I left home. I still hadn't talked to her. While in Vietnam I was preaching one Sunday to a group of guys on our ship about pride and arrogance. That is when I realized how bad I had been toward Mom. I wrote to her and apologized about my arrogance and said I had been blessed in life. I got a letter from her, and she asked why I used the word "blessed." I wrote her back and told her I was now a Christian and that God had blessed me. She wrote me back and said she had become one also! Because I was on a ship in Vietnam, I still hadn't talked to her.

Out of the Box Insights

As I continued talking to God on this canal walk, I received even more insights about my life experiences:

- Mom and I both became followers of Christ because the Lord used each of us to bring the other to him.
- He used our ongoing problems with each other to bring us closer to him over the whole time.
- He used our bad relationship to expose our problems and to bring us closer to each other as a mother and a son.
- God used all these things to reveal his love toward us individually.
- Because of our negative background, the Lord proved his ability to turn it all around to the good.

- All the positive events and changes between us were because of God's love, and it was God's love that we had for each other.

This next insight was a mind-blower! I knew this was why God told me to go for a walk.

- My mother and I received these insights at the same time—me on a long walk along the canal, and she in heaven. They all came after her spirit was in heaven. I could envision her crying in delight toward me, and I thought she might even be able to see me standing on a dirt road at the canal while I was crying in delight with her!

The last insights were these:

- The reality of our experiences has influenced many people and provided fruit for others in our lives.
- This influence is being passed on to my children.
- God reserved these insights for more than forty years before revealing them to me. My mom's death today brought new life to us both! The bad became good!

Within an hour and a half of mom's passing, I realized things I had never connected to before. I was crying loudly in joy. If someone had been on that dirt road with me, they would have called the ambulance. I was exhausted, but not because of sorrow and pain. The insights were overwhelming—the best miracle I had ever experienced.

The week of my mom's death I had been reading and pondering the seventh and eighth chapters of the book of Romans. Their main theme is that for those who love him, God turns all things to the good: "And we know that in all things God works for the good of those who love him, who have been called according to his purpose" (8:28). While suffering may occur during our lives, it does not compare with a life of hope. Nothing can ever prevent God's will for us.

We All Have Stories in Our Lives

I never anticipated that what happened within two hours of my mother's death would be my most life-touching experience. I was crying while walking in comfort. I was wide open to insights about the Father's love—and how he used our family history to bring about spiritual change. God has touched my life in incalculable ways, and he now uses his influence on me to influence others. This is because the good outcomes of my stories were all connected to my mom's life and death. God used them all to prove his love for every one of us.

This book is short compared to all the life stories I have, but I couldn't write them all. We all have stories in our lives, and God wants to use them to bring us closer to him—and to turn all things to the good. We can choose to become followers of Jesus, and then be open to exposing ourselves to bring us closer to God and to others. God is who he is, and he wants to love and care for all of us. Nothing is more real than the promise that God will turn all things to the good for those who love him.

The next pages have photos of where some of my stories took place. Enjoy them!

Use Section 7 to address questions about your life and gain insights for changes. It will also help you remember what you need to remember.

This is the arch I was standing in during the first night's sunset, looking over the whole creation of Arches National Park

This is the camp spot view

This is the arch with two people I asked about
the guy I feared running into

Ian and his sister Kari

Kari's first birthday

Kari's third birthday

Ian and Kari at the
top of our driveway
the first year we lived
on the
Crystal River

Ian and Kari, next to her birthday gift, I made the cabin for her

Ian and Kari loved each other

Ian is holding Casen and his girlfriend Ashley are next to Jason
and Kari, who had colored her hair to black. They are all on
the same spot in photo #11 but it is about 20 years later.
The bushes grew tall and block the river view

My first best photo of my Grandson Casen and me

Casen on the giant lizard

The year 2010 Christmas gift photo of Casen

This is the largest Hot Spring in the world at Glenwood Springs where I
live and spend time with my daughter's family and my son

Kari, Jason and Casen with me in Arizona's Mall

Jason, my son in-law went hiking with me to the top of the Superstition
Mountain in Arizona

July 2011 my daughter and grandson came to Colorado and we
went camping at Lake Irwin and hiked along a river

We also went to the Diamond J Ranch in the mountains in
Colorado where my son is the chef at the ranch and we
camped there and went hiking

My son Ian and I went camping at Spring Canyon Point in Utah

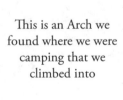

This is an Arch we found where we were camping that we climbed into

Jason, Kari and Casen went hiking with me in Arizona on the Superstition Mountain

This is where my grandson, son-in-law and my daughter went camping with me in Colorado at the Lizard Lake, the first time ever since their marriage. This was also a major event for me and them. A tree limb fell on my back and they had to take me to the emergency room at the hospital. I thought I was going to die

This is Doug Self's family. I took the picture at our dinner time

This was a Christmas time when Doug, Ian and me went shooting

Doug Self and his wife Rebecca and I were at the
North Rim of the Grand Canyon

This is my family at the Superstition Mountain where
I was camping in November 2011

My friend Ken McGraw who was the professional photographer who did the photos for the cover of the book. He was also the friend who sold us the Toyota Camry and knew about the Eagle Premier in the story *Blinded By Good Intentions*

SECTION 7

WORKBOOK

Section 1: In the Beginning

Go back into your history and write out some of the events in your life that had a large impact, good or bad, on you.

_____

_____

_____

_____

_____

_____

_____

What could have been life rules, vows, and commitments that came from these events? Were there good intentions?

_____

_____

_____

_____

_____

_____

_____

_____

What were your motives about those life rules, vows, commitments, and good intentions?

_____

_____

_____

_____

_____

_____

_____

_____

Helpful Tips

Ask God to start revealing his insights about these things. When you think you get some, write them down.

Discuss these concepts with someone you trust who has gotten past their own issues. (Discussing them with someone who is off track may take you further down the wrong path.)

Find some books about others' stories to help you see yours.

Reread the first section of this book a few times to help connect some dots about stories and motives.

Section 2: Insights for Change

What are some life patterns you have to fulfill your life rules, vows, commitments, or intentions?

_____

_____

_____

_____

_____

_____

_____

List some negative comments you have repeatedly heard from others—and any insights about them that may be connected to some of these patterns.

_____

_____

_____

_____

_____

_____

What might be some of your good intentions that are going wrong?

_____

_____

_____

_____

_____

_____

_____

Helpful Tips

Commit some time to gain information from other sources instead of using your time to watch TV, surf the Web, read newspapers, listen to the radio, or other things. *Suggested Authors:* Rick Warren, Greg Boyd, Rob Bell, Larry Crabb, John Eldredge, Chuck Swindoll, Philip Yancey, David Murrow, Donald Miller, Andy Stanley, and Joyce Meyer. Most have podcasts. Just Google their names for access.

Read the books I mentioned. Prioritize reading the Bible for insights.

Bible accounts that connect to this book can be found in Proverbs, Isaiah, Romans, Colossians, 1 Corinthian 13, 2 Peter 1, Ephesians, and Luke.

Go to www.TheOrchardlife.com and download podcasts from pastor Doug Self or the other pastors.

From your list of good intentions, ask others how those intentions seem to be working. Be open to hear, not to defend, what they might say.

Section 3: Solutions Can be the Enemy

What negative thoughts are you replaying? What patterns or processes, which you thought would work, aren't working?

_____

_____

_____

_____

_____

_____

Go back over Section 3, Chapter 5 (Perspectives and Opinions That Are Right and Wrong). Review my list of perspectives, then write down yours.

_____

_____

_____

_____

_____

_____

_____

Who do you want to have a positive influence on? What do you think it will take to influence others, instead of controlling them?

_____

_____

_____

_____

_____

_____

_____

_____

Go on line, search for the phrase "personality test," and take a test. Look at your negative patterns. Consider the consequences of your personality issues that are causing negative consequences.

Section 4: Can You Spare Some Change?

What are some things or events that had a positive effect on your life?

_____

_____

_____

_____

_____

_____

Helpful Tips

Remember and replay good stories. Do not set your mind on the bad.

Maintain a relationship with God as your priority, not those things (such as TV, magazines, and lots more) that tempt us to become preoccupied or waste time.

Choose to be open-minded. Wrestle against excuses and being defensive. Look for a nugget of truth within the bad things people say to you.

Take responsibility for your problems instead of blaming others.

Admit problems to friends, family, and those you want to influence (not to everyone and anyone).

Seek to stand on the middle path instead of being aggressive or passive.

Fight for others' hearts instead of fighting for your wants and needs.

Write your stories about life changes. I wrote mine for my kids!

For more information about Steve White and his life story, visit:
www.BlindedByGoodIntentions.com